DRIFTING YUKON

*living in two worlds with
Yup'ik Eskimo salmon hunters*

DRIFTING YUKON

living in two worlds with
Yup'ik Eskimo salmon hunters

Dan Syljuberget

black hills books

DRIFTING YUKON
©2016 Dan R. Syljuberget

Cover photo by Dan R. Syljuberget
Back cover photo and author's bio photo by Paula R. Collins
All other photography by Dan R. Syljuberget

FIRST U.S. PRINT EDITION

ISBN-13: 978-1-5078-1158-0

Published by Black Hills Books, Rapid City, South Dakota

Book Website
Available from BlackHillsBooks.com
Available from Amazon.com and other book stores

Printed in U.S.A

CONTENTS

ACKNOWLEDGEMENTS

Ralph Waldo Emerson once wrote, "Life is a journey, not a destination." For most of my adult life I have strived to adhere to this simple philosophy.

This book, itself, has had quite the long journey with a number of people who helped along the way. Accordingly, I would like to thank them each for their individual contributions to making this work possible. First, I would like to thank Jane Ochsner Turner and my brother, Mike S. Syljuberget, who have always been there for me. Jane has long been a presence in my world. My brother, Mike, was there in the beginning while Allen and I were college students together in Oregon.

Annalise Zens and Amanda Even retyped the original document into Microsoft Word in 2003 while they were high school students at Hill City School District in the Black Hills in South Dakota. My friend Chuck Landon was an early editor.

For many years after that, this project gathered dust and was nearly forgotten until I shared it with Barb Evenson, a fellow writing enthusiast. I am enormously indebted to Barb, Patti Rudge, Mimi Lancsak, and Bonnie Norrod of Black Hills Books for taking a huge leap of faith with this manuscript.

My coworkers and friends, Ronda Freel and Alex McLean, each gave this work much needed and careful edits. My longtime dear friend and partner, Peg Neal, has seen this work nearly from its zenith many years ago. Her careful scrutiny, edits of the work, and other suggestions resulted in some major revisions.

Finally, without William and Annie, who long have inspired me with their passions for passing on the Yup'ik language and knowledge of Yup'ik traditional ways to the youth of their culture, this project would never have had occurred. William and Annie, thank you for sharing so much of your journeys with me.

EXPLANATIONS

While the places and events in this nonfiction work are factual and real, and take place during the early to mid 1980s, the names of the Green family members have been changed to protect their privacy.

The small public university in Monmouth, Oregon has undergone several names changes over the years. Its present name is Western Oregon University (WOU). In this work, this institution is referred to as Western Oregon State College (WOSC) as that was its name when I attended classes there.

Dan Syljuberget

PART ONE
OREGON

Chapter One

THE LATECOMER

I made it to class early and had time to view the seating situation. This was a fairly new lecture room in a twelve-year-old science building. The seats were a new type to me. They were in long rows with each row on a step and having a single long desk/table extending nearly wall to wall. The chairs were certainly not made for the average uncoordinated person because they required their intended occupants to be gymnasts to climb into them. They were attached to the long desk with a metal bar which pivoted on its attachment underneath the desk when you pulled it out from the desk to attempt to sit in it. The chair also swiveled on the other end. The whole damn thing made you feel as though you were playing with a steel-jawed bear trap that would snap at any moment injuring your hand, knee, or hipbone, and most certainly your modesty as you fumbled around with your books.

On my third attempt, I managed to seat myself with the back of the chair crashing into my hipbones, the metal bar pushing my chair forward so that the edge of the desk stuck in my ribs. There I sat, effectively pinned, and wondered how the hell I was going to get out.

I had strategically picked the seat at the end of the row, close to the door so that I could make a quick exit if necessary; I had a habit of slipping out of classes before the end of the period. I also had a bit of claustrophobia and purposely avoided being trapped in the middle of a long row of people.

By ones, twos, and threes, the students trickled into the lecture room. Nearly all were eighteen and nineteen-year-old freshmen. Physical Science was a required course for all students intending to graduate from Western Oregon State College

(WOSC) with a liberal arts degree. I guessed that there was only one other transfer student, also in his twenties, besides me.

They all seemed to know each other, chattering like frisky otters about future dorm events and the previous night's parties that had kicked off the beginning of their college careers. Coming from a community college where the average student age was around thirty, I felt like I was seated among a bunch of high school students. Restrained by my chair, I was surrounded by the adolescent energy, the mating game was already evident on the first day of college.

These "post-pubes" were wearing the typical costumes of the day for their ages and socioeconomic backgrounds. The guys wore preppy oxford cloth shirts or cotton sweaters above ratty, holey, faded Levi 501 blue jeans, and white basketball shoes, usually hi-tops that were not laced through the top three or four eyelet pairs. The bottoms of their jeans looked as if they couldn't quite decide whether to slouch in the tops of the shoes or hang over them, resulting in a little of both.

Some of the girls, wearing wool-blended skirts and sweaters or pant outfits, dressed better than boys. Most looked older than their male peers. Many of the boys looked as if their faces had never needed to know a razor's edge.

Although I was enjoying the dynamics of the scene, I felt a bit out of place. I was only one or two years older but with a markedly receding hairline, full beard, and glasses I looked five to seven years older. I had been working fulltime the last two years as a short-order cook while taking part-time community college classes; I felt older. My feet were in old Redwing lace-up work boots and I wore a faded, red hoody over a T-shirt and Levi 501 jeans. My jeans were the same kind as the other young men, but I wore mine a size or two looser, preferring comfort over sex appeal.

One young man entered the room wearing Levis so tight that I couldn't figure out how he put his shoes on that morning unless he had left his jeans unbuttoned to do so. He must have put on those super-tight jeans hoping to make a good impression on one of the young ladies that might be possibly waiting for a pantsful such as he.

A short middle-aged woman wearing a white smock came into the room. Thinking she might be a custodian of some sort, I looked around while sniffing delicately at the air wondering if someone had lost his or her cookies resulting from a couple of shots of a favorite beverage this morning to help ease the hangover from last night. But then I noticed that she dragged a chair to the front of the room near the professor's podium and seated herself. While I was wondering what she was doing, a young man came into the room, glided up to a row below

4

me, and endeavored to get into a chair using the one-handed method of pulling the chair out of the long desk while holding his books and belongings with the other hand. In his case, however, the exasperating chair rebelled, as it had for most others, causing him to clatter his books and things to the floor.

In the diminishing silence—which quickly followed the loud disturbance effectively ending intellectual discussions of "who laid whom," or "who got fuckin' trashed last night"—a young lady, who apparently knew the young man, assisted him in gathering his books. He spoke to her in a halting manner with slurred consonants and vowels that came out either very guttural or very nasal—making his speech difficult to understand. He was deaf, yet somewhere, sometime, in his life, he had managed to learn to speak. She accepted his thanks and agreed to help him take notes during class. He seated himself, this time using both hands to handle the chair after putting his books and things on the desk. Then using his fluent first language, ASL (American Sign Language), he signed to the middle-aged woman with the white smock seated at the front of the room, and she signed back to him in ASL. I had never been in a class with a working interpreter and was interested in this enlightenment in case the professor was a boring lecturer.

By now, the people entering the class were the last minute stragglers, rushing to class in order to not be late on the first day. A very smartly dressed woman, whom I judged to be close to my age, came into the room. She was tall and slender, and wore a long black wool dress coat. Her Highness walked up the stairs to my row, choosing the only empty seat in the row, the one next to me, she took off her coat to reveal a white silk blouse and maroon wool blended slacks. She looked exceptionally striking and very mature. I felt a genuine physical attraction to Her Highness and hoped she might notice the obvious maturity and ruggedness of the balding, bespectacled young man seated next to her. Hmmm....

After Her Highness sat down, with ease I might add, she turned slowly around to my direction. Dark, careful waves of hair caressed her delicate, white face. I felt my heart lurch a little and hoping to sound suave and debonair, I said, "Wow—nice outfit."

Her eyes briefly caught mine when I spoke and they showed no warmth. As she continued to slowly turn around to the person directly behind her, she snapped hurriedly at me, "Oh-thanks-I-work-at-Nordstrom's," indicating sharply that because she worked at a nice clothing store, she had nice clothes.

I quickly noticed that the person behind her she had intended to talk to behind her was Mr. Tight Jeans. He still had that sly "I'm a stud" grin on his face. He asked her if she worked last night. She answered "yes" and then blathered excitedly remarking with glee, "I heard you got really shit-faced last night!"

After she brushed off my "opening," I instantly felt devastated—and red-faced, thinking she must have overlooked the—um—obvious maturity and ruggedness and noticed only the balding head. Maybe instead of suave and debonair, she thought I was trying to be a come-on to her. Maybe I was. But as she flirted on with Studly, she didn't seem as mature and attractive as she did before she opened her mouth. She was just like the other eighteen-year-old cliquey Sally-Rallys in the room flirting eagerly among themselves, and with their stud-muffin boyfriends-to-be, discussing parties and "who-was-with-whom." She was simply a little better dressed because she had a job in a high-class ladies clothing store.

Yes, I felt a little jealous and a little out of place. I didn't fit in with this crowd at all. Even the hearing-impaired boy seemed to know everyone. But then I really didn't want to "fit-in." While on the one hand I felt like the "oddball" in the group, on the other hand I was enjoying the multistage dramas and mating game around me. The professor had entered by this time, closed the door, organized his thoughts and was just about to begin his introductory speech when the door opened once more.

The last latecomer gently closed the door behind him and after one quick glance with his dark eyes seeing every face of the juvenile bunch staring at him, he then bulled forward to the closest empty seat which was the last chair in the front row, three rows straight down from me. When he came into the room, I was immediately curious about his ethnic origin; my thoughtful questions didn't come up with any positive answers. Hispanic? No. Arabic? Neither slender nor hairy enough. Native American? Perhaps. But the Native Americans that I had grown up in South Dakota were taller and a more slightly built than this man.

He was very stocky, about five feet four inches tall with a huge torso of heavy rounded shoulders, a barrel-chest, and a belly on top of short, bowed legs. He must have weighed close to two hundred pounds, heavy for such a short-statured man. His belly protruded out well beyond the top button of his Levis, but it didn't look floppy and stuck out only a little more than his heavy chest.

Black hair fell over his ears. This combined with dark-framed glasses of photo-gray lenses still darkened from the outside light and a little black mustache sporting his upper lip gave him a slightly menacing look.

Even without having met him, I felt a little sorry for the latecomer, anticipating the arduous task he unknowingly faced of managing his bulk into the wicked chair in front of the now watchful assembly of young Anglo-American faces. But he seemed quite in control of his resources and demonstrated a possible mechanical aptitude by seating himself with minimal disturbance.

Again he shot a quick glance around the room, this time from his seated position effectively providing me with a full view of his profile. His round wide face matched his build, and he had a thrusting jaw perhaps caused by an underbite, which further complemented his bulldog "don't mess with me" appearance. Yet, he retained a remarkably inquisitive aura. While his eyes, at first, appeared cold and sharp when looking at him face-on through his glasses, as he looked to his right, I could see through the unshielded right eye in the little space between the edge of his glasses frames and face—an eye that revealed an inquisitive nature.

He cleared his throat nervously and turned back to face the professor who was about ready to begin. The latecomer sat there waiting with his thick trunk hunched with tension. I could almost feel, as he may have, with the little hairs on the back of his neck sticking out resulting from the curious roomful of piercing eyes behind him glued in his direction. He was the only non-white person in the room, and was six to eight years older than the next oldest student in the room—me.

In the brief moments that had elapsed since he entered the room and seated himself, I felt I had grown to know him a little. At least if I hadn't, I knew that I would soon.

Chapter Two
THE MEETING

During the remainder of that first class period and for most of the rest of the day, I thought little else about the latecomer on that very first day of college. Shortly before my last class of the day, I was scurrying to the student union to get a milkshake for my growling stomach when I was nearly bowled over by a very fat boy on a bicycle. He was about ten-years-old and smiled sheepishly. His broad, dark face, and hair reminding me of the latecomer in the morning class. He spoke a "sorry" in a raspy pre-adolescent male voice, dropped his bike, and waddled into the student union.

When I arrived at my last class of the day, *Culture and Society*, with milkshake in hand, the only other students were seated at the back of the classroom next to each other: the black-haired bulky fellow I had observed in the *Physical Science* class that morning and a woman who closely resembled him both in looks and build. I smiled and they both gave me the warmest smiles I'd ever seen. I opened up things with, "My name is Dan. I believe you are in another of my classes."

"Yes. *Physical Science*. I'm Allen and this is Clara."

By this time, my curiosity was peaking. They looked so much alike that they had to be brother and sister. I thought it would be a little rude to ask that if they were really a married couple, so I asked, "Are you two married?" which stirred both to hearty laughter.

"No. We're brother and sister."

I seated myself next to Allen, and the three of us chatted for several minutes while the classroom filled with students. I learned that they were Yup'ik Eskimos from Mountain Village on the lower Yukon River in Alaska and that they, like me, were both planning on becoming teachers. Clara, the older of the two, had attended Western Oregon State College (WOSC) the year before. Allen was a transfer student from the University of Alaska in Fairbanks.

Later I learned that the word "Yup'ik" refers to a language that a specific group of roughly 16,000 Eskimos speak. Yup'ik is also used to refer to Eskimos living in western Alaska just as the word "French" is used to describe the people living in France. In the Eskimo Raven legends dealing with the origin of the world and life, the creator Raven calls the first man, Yup'ik, "a true man" (Morgan 98). Later definitions of Yup'ik are similar but eliminate the sexist generic "man." The Yup'ik Eskimo Dictionary defines "Yup'ik" as "a real person" (Jacobson 416).

At one point during our introductory discussion, a young voice, half-spoken and half whispered, came from the hallway into the classroom urging, "Clara!" When I looked toward the door, I noticed the young fat boy who had nearly killed me with his bicycle earlier. The resemblance between the boy and the two seated next to me was uncanny. "Later ...after class... three o'clock," Clara spoke to the boy in a deliberate way.

Allen turned to me chuckling, "He probably wants money for candy."

Clara proudly added, to clear up my obvious confusion, "That's my boy Donnie."

While talking with Allen and Clara, I observed that Allen spoke very quickly with no hesitancy, but Clara spoke very slowly and carefully almost as if she were interpreting what to say in her mind. Later I learned they were both bilingual. They could read, write, and speak in two languages. Yup'ik was their first language and they learned English while attending a Catholic mission school. Clara's ten-year old son, Donnie, spoke English fluently and knew only a smattering of Yup'ik words.

Chapter Three
SETTLING IN

M y younger brother, Mike, and I shared an apartment together in Corvallis, Oregon during the first year I attended Western Oregon State College (WOSC). Then Corvallis was a hip-happening university town with a population of about 45,000 with roughly 17,000 attending Oregon State University (OSU). Classes were huge. Sometimes numbering in the hundreds, you can quickly feel like a number yourself as you seemed to fade into obscurity amid the masses.

Monmouth, the small college town north of Corvallis, by comparison, was much smaller. A stroll down Monmouth Avenue through the middle of WOSC's small campus may bring dozens of hellos and waves from those passing by, whether they knew you or not. With a small student population of around 2500, it didn't take long to recognize most of those people waving and greeting you between classes on the sidewalk.

Mike commuted daily by bicycle about three-quarter of a mile south from our apartment to his engineering courses at OSU, while I commuted daily by car twenty-eight miles north to my education courses at WOSC in Monmouth.

I made many new friends, but grew to know Allen, Clara, and Donnie quite well almost to the point of being considered a member of their little family unit. I felt an increasing pull towards Monmouth and away from Corvallis. Mike was my only sibling and we have always been very close brothers. At the time in our lives, however, the only other thing we shared, besides being close members of the same family, was an apartment and the living expenses that came with it. His life, at the moment, was OSU in Corvallis while mine was WOSC in Monmouth at WOSC. I worked part time at WOSC's library, took classes, socialized with new-found friends between classes, and worked in Monmouth.

Allen was born in 1956, making him at least six years older then me. Clara was older than Allen, in her early thirties, and had attended WOSC the previous year. Her son, ten-year old Donnie, who always traveled wherever Clara went, took great pleasure in showing Allen and me places of interest in Monmouth. These places were of high importance to Donnie and usually dealt with entertainment or food, so Allen and I were soon exposed to the video machines in the basement of the College Center (student union), The Cubby Hole, a sandwich shop on the main floor of the college, and Kwang Chau Restaurant, located just to the south of WOSC's campus featuring Donnie's favorite meal, sweet and sour pork.

Although Allen and I grew to enjoy frequenting The Cubby Hole and Kwang Chau, we never developed appetites for Pac-man and Asteroids video games. Nevertheless, during the duration that Donnie and Clara lived in Monmouth, whenever Donnie was nowhere-to-be-found, a good guess on his whereabouts would be in the basement of the College Center playing Pac-man – often with a college student. Since WOSC had its own elementary school on campus, elementary students were a common sight on campus during after-school hours.

During the first several months that we attended WOSC together, patterns developed with all of us. Allen, Clara, Donnie, and I attended our respective classes during the mornings and early afternoons and then met at their apartment sometime during the late afternoon to loaf around, to study, or to plan a trip to Salem some fifteen miles east for shopping, or to nearby Basket Slough National Wildlife Refuge for exploring, hiking, and wildlife observation.

Chapter Four
GETTING ALLEN A VEHICLE

Because neither Clara nor Allen owned an automobile, I was solicited every so often to drive them to nearby Salem for shopping. During one such occasion while walking through Lancaster Mall, Allen made an announcement to me.

"Dan…I need a vehicle."

Three things struck me with this statement. First, both Allen and Clara always directed statements and questions to me with a loud, sharp "Dan," to get my attention. This attention-getter was followed by a pause of silence, and then came the statement or question.

The second thing I noted was Allen's word choice "vehicle" rather than "car" or "some wheels," both of which I was used to. Later, I learned that "sno-go" or "snow-machine" meant "snowmobile." "Kicker" refers to the outboard motor for a boat. "Vehicle" always meant car, truck, or automobile.

What struck me the most about his "I need a vehicle" declaration was that I would probably have to teach him to drive. How much did he know? Could he drive a car? What did he know about our traffic laws?

"Well, you'll have to get a driver's license first. Have you ever driven a car before?

"No—but I've driven my dad's Ford pickup truck."

"Is it a shift or automatic?" He'd have to learn in my Mazda, which had a manual transmission.

"Yeh—it's a shift. I don't like automatics."

"Neither do I. Maybe it's just a matter of you getting used to roads and rules around here. You'll have to pass a written exam, vision exam, and a driving exam in order to get your license."

"Yeh—okay—Dan—that sounds good."

About a week later I found myself in the role of driver's education instructor. From the beginning of Allen's first driving lesson, it was clear that he knew how to handle a car. Also clear was the realization that he knew very little about rules of the road. In fact the average eight-year-old Oregon kid knew more about traffic rules than Allen did when we first started his driving lessons. He had seen traffic signal lights in Fairbanks and Anchorage but needed me to explain that the red light means "stop" before the intersection, "green" signaled proceed through the intersection, and "yellow" meant caution the red light will shortly follow.

Fortunately, Monmouth was a quiet little town with easy access to several county and state highways with sparse traffic. After several weeks, Allen and I felt he was ready for his test. He passed the written and visual exams with ease, but was unable to take the driving test because I could not find any proof of liability insurance in the Mazda. A second attempt to take the test was thwarted due to a faulty taillight. When Allen finally was able to take his driving test, he failed three times in a row.

Nevertheless, Allen began looking for vehicles for sale and bought a 1969 Ford F100 pickup from a private owner long before he passed his driving exam. The pickup was old but in excellent condition. It had a straight six engine and a manual transmission which Allen preferred.

Chapter Five
THANKSGIVING

By November, Allen, Clara, and I had grown quite close. It seemed logical to invite them to spend Thanksgiving with my family in Silverton, Oregon. I arranged with my dad to borrow the station wagon so we could all drive to Silverton together.

Allen, Clara, and Donnie Green had never met my parents, nor my aunt and uncle from Seattle who would also be spending Thanksgiving in Silverton with us. I prepped both the Greens and my parents on meeting each other. It was up to my parents to prep Uncle Floyd and Aunt Max to meet a Yup'ik Eskimo family. I didn't know how my parents, or my aunt and uncle would react to them. We all decided to just let things happen naturally. As we drove, I told Allen, Clara, and Donnie about my home.

My parent's home was a lovely, four bedroom, split-level house which sat halfway up a wooded hill on the edge of town. About two acres of natural Oregon woods came with the house when my folks bought it four years before. The woods on both sides of the property were undeveloped as well—left to nature—so the whole wooded area behind the house totaled about thirty acres of thick strands of fir and oak trees, mossy rocks and logs, ferns, and wild blackberry bushes.

An old bachelor of Norwegian ancestry named Nestor owned most of the surrounding acreage. He lived in an old shack at the base of the hill since his infancy in 1908. Nestor's major daily pursuit was to amble in his ancient Ford pickup truck to Safeway to buy three loaves of day-old bread. His evening activity was to feed his wild raccoon friends which inhabited the woods. Every night, a few minutes before sundown, a toothless and raspy "Here Coony, Coony" could be heard echoing up the hill towards us as Nestor called to the wild raccoons in the area to come for his bread handouts. Some of the raccoons became so used to the old man and his ways that they would follow him into his house for more bread.

The raccoons could be viewed nightly in our own backyard on their trek either down to Nestor's yard or back up the hill from their feeding. We also often saw skunks, possum, and deer very close to the house. The deer could be seen any time of day. My mother still has photos of deer touching the basement windows to peer in at the two-legged creatures on the other side.

Allen, Clara, and Donnie were used to seeing myriads of waterfowl, moose, beaver, and muskrats back in their home in Alaska. Their curiosity heightened along with their nervousness as we drove the ninety minute drive from Monmouth to Silverton while I told them about my home.

While visiting my family, Allen was the most open and talkative of the three. Clara was painfully shy, talking carefully, only when asked a question. She drank in everything from the new faces, to different items in the house, and frequently her wide eyes met mine and Allen's for reassurance. Donnie basked in the adult attention one receives as being the only child present at a gathering of adults.

They had previously eaten most of the varieties of typical Thanksgiving fare except the cranberry sauce which Mom made by reducing frozen cranberries into a mixture of water and sugar into a sauce. Allen declared that the cranberries would probably make for a good home remedy for the flu. The texture, taste, and color may have reminded him of a cough syrup mixture he had taken as a child.

Viewing the raccoons during their evening ritual down the hill to Nestor's for bread drew an interesting response from the Green family, whose culture is harvesting as much of one's diet as possible from the land. Allen suggested that I get my shotgun and shoot one so he could skin it and cook it so we could all see how it tasted.

The Friday after Thanksgiving traditionally marks the event of putting up a Christmas tree in my family. We used an artificial tree because of family allergies, but our tree was always the most beautiful I had ever seen. The Greens loved decorating the tree. Clara, smiling with wonder, gazed at the tree with its lights creating a soft glow around the pine cones and hand crocheted snowflakes. Most of the Christmas decorations throughout the house were hand-made by my mother. I think that Allen, Clara, and Donnie were a little homesick and looked forward to Christmas break when they could return home to Mountain Village and their own family.

The Greens were unconditionally accepted by my family. They in turn were glad to know my family. Dan's family. Allen, Clara, and I were already starting to function as our own surrogate family. In the following two years, as my own blood family disintegrated by my parents' separation and divorce, Allen, Clara, and Donnie became the only family of which I felt part.

Chapter Six
DRINKING AND DRIVING

Having grown up in South Dakota, I was familiar with the stories that circulated about Native American people's addiction and abuse of alcohol. My family and I moved from South Dakota to Oregon when I was sixteen years old. The same criticism in Oregon existed, with racist overtones, aimed at Hispanics. Early the fall of my first year at WOSC, while I was commuting back and forth between Monmouth and Corvallis, some of our fellow students who noticed my close friendship with Allen made remarks to me such as: "Oh, an Eskimo. They drink like fish and get really crazy."

I knew that Allen and Clara had experienced the effects of alcoholism in their family. The oldest brother, Leonard, a tall man for a Yup'ik Eskimo, came home a very confused and frustrated individual after his tour in Vietnam. The culture shock that he experienced must have been incredible. When Leonard traveled to boot camp in congested California (in the early 1960s) Mountain Village didn't even have running water or electricity. From there, he was shipped overseas to the jungles of Vietnam. Southwestern Alaska, by contrast, has very few trees; most of the vegetation on the tundra reaches a mere six inches in height.

When Leonard came home from Vietnam, he drowned his confusion in a bottle and took his frustrations out by beating his family members. Frequently Allen, the youngest boy, the shortest statured one, and the one most favored by their father, was the target. Allen told Leonard that he would kill him if he ever beat him again. After the incident, Leonard left Allen alone. To this day there exists an uneasy peace between the two.

I was slower than others at WOSC to recognize Allen's drinking problem. Perhaps part of it was blind denial. My friend? Perhaps it was my limited exposure to alcoholism and alcohol itself. Except for an alcoholic uncle who died of a heart attack at age 57, no one in my immediate family drank more than occasionally. I hardly touched alcohol myself until I was well into my late teens.

My first inkling of Allen's drinking problem came during the first Thanksgiving break when we visited a bar in Salem, Oregon. On that occasion, the barmaid had asked Allen what kind of house he lived in when she learned that he was an Eskimo. His reply was, "a three-story igloo." When we left the bar, Allen was quite drunk. He had consumed three mixed drinks in the time I had one beer. He wanted to find another tavern. I had to nab him by the shirt to pull him back onto the sidewalk after he tried to stroll out into a busy street. It took a lot of gentle persuasion to get his mind off wanting more booze.

Flashbacks of mutual acquaintances, women that both Allen and I knew at WOSC, kept hammering in my mind. WOSC was mostly a teacher's college. The female population far outnumbered the male population. Naturally many of our friends were women. While steering Allen towards the car in Salem, I remembered at least two separate incidents when women that Allen and I both knew approached me with complaints that Allen had come to their apartments drunk, loud, and obnoxious the previous night.

Allen's entrance into the bottle roughly paralleled the acquisition of the pickup truck and obtaining his instructional driving permit. He was still unable to pass his driving test, so nearly all the time Allen drove illegally during his first year at WOSC. The Oregon driving manual states that those people with an instruction permit can not legally drive without the presence of a licensed driver in the vehicle with them. But Allen drove without me anyway. He drove Clara and Donnie to the grocery store in Monmouth. When he got frustrated and confused he drove to nearby towns of Independence or Dallas to get drunk.

Monmouth is the only dry town in the state of Oregon. The town legend provides a reason as to why Monmouth is dry. The story is that back in the 1800s, a local wealthy family deeded some land to the college and forced an agreement with the college that if booze was ever commercially sold in Monmouth, the college would return ownership of the land back to descendants of the family.

Whatever the reasons, Monmouth is dry. It is a small obstacle for those wanting to buy alcohol. A town called Independence is only four miles to the east, Dallas is ten miles to the northwest, and Salem is fifteen miles to the northeast.

Regrettably, by teaching Allen to drive, assisting him in getting his license, and assisting him in finding a vehicle, I enabled him access to alcohol. So, in essence, I contributed a great deal to his drinking problem.

I drank with Allen only one time after the incident in Salem, Oregon. It was a week or two later that Allen, my brother, and I met at a bar in nearby Independence, Oregon. Allen was picked up and ticketed for "Driving While under the Influence." I finally began questioning Clara about Allen's drinking and learned that when he was frustrated, he would disappear for many hours and return home drunk, sometimes violently drunk and always frightening Clara and Donnie.

So I tried talking to Allen, to get at the roots of why he drank. It is well known that college students like to party and drink heavily, but Allen left town alone and sober—and drove home alone and drunk, often. He did it more often in actuality than I believed at first. He described feelings of frustration as though he didn't belong with his people back home in Mountain Village, Alaska, or fit in with the college group in Monmouth, Oregon. He considered himself an oddity. Sometimes, the motivator for him to disappear for many hours would be something specific like getting a low mark on a test when he had high expectations of getting a high grade, or an open criticism from a professor. The booze became a cycle. He drank when he was depressed, then performed poorly with a hangover, and became depressed when he performed poorly.

Finally, on a late night return from Dallas, Allen passed out behind the wheel of his truck. The truck veered into a field. When the truck hit the approach, it rolled over on the left side, the driver's side. Allen woke up in the Dallas hospital some hours later with only bruises, scrapes, and scratches. Perhaps the extreme state of his inebriation relaxed him enough so that his body did not tense during the accident, thereby helping to prevent broken bones or internal injuries. Perhaps, too, Allen's bulky-build, 5'4" and two hundred pounds at the time—served to pad him in the crash.

Clara and I drove to the hospital the next day to see Allen. We weren't sure how to deal with him. After his D.W.I., he had been attending classes required of him by the State of Oregon on alcohol, driving, and self-discipline. Some of the material discussed at the class made sense to him and he seemed to benefit from the group discussions when other problem drinkers, like him, shared some of their difficulties. It made him feel a little less like an oddity. But he still obviously had not yet accepted the fact that he also had a drinking problem. The accident was proof of this.

He was awake and alert when we entered his room. We knew beforehand that he had survived the accident with only minor injuries, so I was not worried for him. I was mad at him. I didn't say anything to Allen about his stupidity while I was there—not in front of Clara. And that was what Allen expected me to do. I was so mad at him that I wasn't going to give him the satisfaction of doing anything he expected me to do. I only asked him a few brief questions as to the extent of his bruises and when he would be released.

His answers were a little hard to understand through fat, distorted, and stitched lips. I did not look at him for long. I did not smile at him. When I did look at him, I glared at him with my eyes. My questions were quick, curt, and blunt. He avoided looking at me as much as possible, with only occasional darting glances at my face. He knew that I was furious and disappointed with him. He waited for the chew-out session that he never received.

Allen was released from the Dallas Hospital the next day. On the way home from the hospital, he insisted on stopping to look at the remains of his truck at the junkyard where it had been towed. Both of us were aghast when we saw the extent of the damage. The truck would never be driven again. The front left side was smashed. The hood had been sprung somehow from the vehicle and was now loosely covering the engine, sticking further out than the engine compartment. The left door and left front fender were bashed. The left window and left mirror were both missing. The whole truck body sat twisted on its chassis. It truly was a miracle that Allen survived the accident with as few injuries as he did.

Later, as we were on our way back toward Monmouth, we found the point where Allen had left the road. We stopped the Mazda, and got out to follow the trail left by the out-of-control pickup down along the ditch. We found the broken side-mirror close to the field approach from the highway crossing the ditch—the place where the truck hit, stopped, and rolled over onto its left side. Allen was very somber when he picked it up and turned it over in his hands. "I'm going to keep this to remember what I did," he said as he looked at his reflection in the broken mirror.

Chapter Seven
SEPARATION

With the loss of his pickup, Allen and Clara had no transportation; Allen had no means of traveling to Independence or Dallas to get drunk. As the school year came to a close, Allen pestered me to fly with him, Clara, and Donnie to their home in Mountain Village, Alaska for the summer. They told me that most of their summers were spent at Fish Camp, a family camp made on a long narrow island in the middle of the Yukon, about thirty-five miles downstream from Mountain Village.

At their fish camp, which apparently most Yup'ik families had, Allen, two of his brothers, Leonard and Clyde, and their father, Joe, fished commercially for salmon, each in their own boats. The salmon were caught in gill nets as the boats drift downriver to intercept the fish fighting their way against the current upriver to spawn. Allen declared, "Dan. You'll be my deckhand."

I desperately wanted to go with them to Alaska that summer, but knew that I couldn't. I didn't have a decent sleeping bag, adequate clothing for commercial fishing including rubber-knee-high boots, and no money for airfare. Allen asked me only a few weeks before the end of the school term and I needed more than two weeks to prepare myself mentally, financially, and to outfit myself for living on a remote island in the middle of the lower Yukon River. I knew from past conversations with Allen and Clara that very few white people lived in the area. Although Allen and Clara viewed me as family, how would other Yup'iks, who did not know me from a bale of hay, and whose few encounters with white men were usually negative associations in the form of bootleggers, drug pushers, slick business profiteers, and other derelicts that leeched off their society, view me? Allen and Clara told me that the white man was not generally regarded in a positive way.

I needed to know, with more certainty, how Allen would handle alcohol while in Alaska, so I told him that I couldn't go, that I needed more time to plan, purchase supplies, and save for the trip. Allen and Clara were disappointed. Allen protested. I told him that we had the whole school year to plan for next summer. They finally agreed and asked me to drive them up to the airport in Portland for their trip home for the summer.

I borrowed my dad's station wagon again to drive the Greens up to the Portland airport roughly forty-five miles northeast of Monmouth. Throughout the school year, Clara acquired a number of houseplants and decided to take three of them with her back to Alaska to give to her mother. Houseplants are hard to come by in rural Alaska.

As Alaskan Eskimos, whose concern for time is mainly seasonal and following the migrations of waterfowl and salmon—as opposed to our servitude to the hours and minutes on the clock due to our rigid schedules—Clara and Allen were notoriously late for classes, meetings, appointments, and scheduled air flight take-offs. They have never really learned to budget their time so that they would not be late. Such was the case of their end-of-the-school-year departure for Portland.

By the time we were loaded in the car in Monmouth, complete with the plants that Clara intended to hand-carry through the entire flight, and drove to the airport in Portland, we stopped in the unloading parking area right outside the main doors of the airport only seven minutes before their flight was scheduled to depart. After checking in their tickets and baggage, only two minutes remained and the terminal was on the other side of the airport!

We were a comical group racing through the airport to get to the terminal before the flight left. Allen was far in the lead, racing to get to the terminal. Clara followed about twenty yards behind with her arms loaded with a plant, carry-on bags, and jacket. Donnie would have been even with his mother in the race to the terminal, except that he intermittently kept dropping a cap, a comic book, or bag of chips out of his loosely packed armload and had to stop, to side-step back to pick up the lost items. I followed about twenty yards behind Donnie carrying two of Clara's plants.

Finally, Allen reached the terminal to show the attendant their tickets and hollered for we stragglers to hurry up. When I finally made it, they adjusted their loads to accommodate the plants I had been carrying and said a very quick goodbye. Then they boarded the plane. It was too fast a goodbye for the friendships, feelings, and experiences we shared over the past nine months. Then, they boarded the plane. Miraculously, the mad, hell-bent-for-election dash to the terminal was a success.

Almost immediately after they boarded, as if the pilots had been waiting for the Green family, the plane moved away from the gateway, taxied down the runway and lifted off. It was going to be a long summer without them. My thoughts would be with them wondering what and how they were doing for the next three months.

Chapter Eight
TRANSITION AND BRAWLING

The summer brought several changes for Mike and me. We moved back to our parent's home in Silverton, Oregon. I returned to my previous job deep-frying onion rings and fries, broiling hamburgers, and microwaving sandwiches at the local A&W. Mike moved irrigation pipe for a local farmer. Neither of us was able to receive any financial aid grants for the upcoming school year.

Mike was a little burned out after his fist year in pre-engineering and decided that he would take a year off from school and work. Mike landed a full-time night job at Roth's IGA grocery store in nearby Independence receiving freight and restocking shelves. I took out a student loan and lined up three part-time jobs at WOSC for the school year. We decided to share an apartment in Monmouth near the campus so that I could walk to school and my jobs and he could drive the four miles to work. As it turned out we found an apartment right across the street from the Greens.

In late August, soon after they settled back in their apartment for the upcoming school year, Allen expressed interest in buying another pickup truck. The previous May he had finally passed his driving test using my Mazda, so he was a fully licensed driver now. But with a D.W.I. and an accident, he had already established a poor driving record. He settled on another Ford. This 1980 F100 was bright orange with chrome mag wheels and a four-speed manual transmission. It was a sharp vehicle and fun to drive.

We all settled into our various roles during the early months of the school year. Mike would sleep during the day and work at night, and the rest of us resumed our college student lives. Basically our lives picked up where they left off at the end of the previous school year. Clara was in her final year of college, a very intense year involving much time in the classroom and eventually student teaching. Having finished our liberal arts core curriculum and beginning our Elementary Education block courses, Allen and I were considered juniors by the registrar. We continued with our sojourns to the coast and to Basket Slough National Wildlife Refuge. We also continued with our long discussions on the differences and similarities of Yup'ik Eskimo and Anglo-American cultures. Through Allen, I became acquainted with other Alaskan natives on campus. Through me, Allen became familiar with many other people and cultures on campus.

Gradually, through the course of the year, I learned more and more about life in Mountain Village, Alaska, and their summer family Yukon River fish camp. As I mentally prepared myself for the next summer's adventures, I slowly accumulated the supplies that I would need: a thick sleeping bag, wool sweaters, hats, rubber knee-high boots, fishing gloves, rain coat, rain pants, and parka. But as I prepared myself for the bush of Yup'ik Eskimo Alaska, and as Allen and Clara continued to prepare me for the trip, I wondered if I would really be going, for soon after Allen bought his second truck, his drinking began again.

Late one Friday night, a rare night that Mike was off work and at home, I received an urgent call from Clara.

"Dan...Allen's at Professor Gutierez's house and you need to bring him home. He's drunk." Dr. Gutierez was a professor of sociology at WOSC.

"How'd he get there?"

"I don't know. Professor Gutierez just called and said Allen was there and that someone should come and get him because he is too drunk to drive. Gutierez took his keys away from him."

When I arrived at the Independence address Clara had given me, I found a smiling, sober Dr. Gutierez, and a very drunk Allen. His glasses were off and lying on the coffee table in front of him. His eyes were glazed and almost shut. His bulldog jaw jutted out further than ever before so that when his head bobbed forward in his stupor; his chin actually touched his chest. Gutierez explained quietly while continuing to smile: "It's partly my fault he's like this. When I ran into him downtown, he was quite loaded. I told him that if he gave me his keys, he could come with me to my house for some tequila. He's had several shots. I'll keep his keys for tonight so that you won't have any problems with him."

We put Allen's glasses on, maneuvered his shoes on and supported him to my car. After we settled him inside, Gutierez bid us goodnight. I thanked him and we drove away. Immediately Allen started acting up. The four-mile-drive back to the Green's apartment turned out to be the longest four miles I've ever had to drive and preceded one of the longest and most stressful nights of my life.

He began by hollering "Where's my fucking truck" over and over at the top of his lungs in my tiny Mazda. To further emphasize his questions, he swung his arms, beating the window with his right fist and me with his left. It made for very difficult driving.

As we neared his apartment, he changed his tune slightly. He thought I had stolen his keys, which terrifically enraged him and caused him to continue flailing his arms about the interior of the Mazda. He cursed me at the top of his lungs all the way home.

Finally as we pulled up to his apartment complex, I jumped out, scooted around the car to open Allen's door, pressed down the lock and pushed him back in the car, effectively locking him in.

I burst in through Clara's apartment door and answered her "Where's Allen?" with "locked in my car" and I told her to call Mike to tell him to come over as soon as he could. I weighed only 143 pounds at the time; Allen outweighed me by over fifty pounds so I needed help in manhandling my drunk, violent friend from the car to the apartment. I told Clara, "I can't handle him by myself. You and Donnie grab some blankets and go over to my place."

I ran back to the car, unlocked Allen's door, and tried helping him out. But he started in with his ranting again. "Where's my fucking keys? You took my fucking keys—I want my fucking truck—give me my keys you little fucker."

With that he took a swing at me but lost his balance when I dodged him and he fell into a bush. As he lay there, I paused for a few seconds before helping him up. I noticed that Allen's disturbance had awoken many of the people in the little court of apartments huddled around the small parking lot. Most of them were at their doors and windows watching the scene.

I pulled Allen up and together we gained a few steps towards the apartment door before he started another tirade. By the time that began, my dependable brother Mike arrived, and between the two of us, we managed to steer Allen into his apartment.

After Mike closed the door of the apartment behind us, we both relaxed a little, feeling a bit better now that Allen was safely inside. That was a mistake, for as soon as we loosened our holds on Allen, he broke away, ran over to Donnie's bike, picked it up with one hand and chucked it at least twelve feet across the room. While Mike and I stared at each other in disbelief, Allen grasped a circular table, with a hand on each side, picked it up and sailed it over toward the couch.

As this happened, there was a knock at the door. When Mike opened the door to see who it was, Allen charged outside right into the arms of two on-duty Monmouth police officers. Apparently one of the neighbors, who had witnessed Allen's and my little tussle in the parking lot, had called the police. The two officers, noticing that both Mike and I were sober, asked if we needed help—that someone had reported a disturbance. I answered, "No, we think we can handle him but we'll give you a call if we can't."

Mike approached Allen from the back and wrapped his very long sinewy arms around Allen's barrel chest, effectively pinning his arms, and dragged him back into the apartment, and sat down on the couch with Allen seated in front of him. I closed the door after saying goodnight to the officers and wondered how, if ever, we would get Allen settled down for the night. I walked casually over toward the couch and laid down slowly on the floor in front of Mike and Allen, like I was going to sleep. "Gee, Allen, aren't you sleepy? I'm really sleepy. Let's go to bed."

I repeated my little attempt at "setting a good example" when I could see him relax in Mike's arms. Allen's head bobbed forward with his chin against his chest and eyes closed. He mumbled, "Yah. Let's go to bed."

Mike relaxed his arms and we both breathed a sigh of relief. Suddenly, however, Allen remembered his anger, bolted out of Mike's loosened arms, sprang off the couch and into the kitchen, nearly squashing me in the process, while continuing his "where's my fucking truck" routine. He tried to tip the refrigerator over but in his drunken state and short stature, thankfully, he couldn't quite get enough leverage. Instead he tore open the door, grabbed a turkey still in its plastic wrap, and twirled it around his head like he meant to lob it either at one of us or across the room.

With this turn of events, I became very angry and stormed into the kitchen hollering, "Shut up Allen! We're tired of messing with you. We want to go to bed. It's three o'clock in the fucking morning. You better get to bed too!"

He came after me with the intention of hurting me. I figured that if he was going to chase me, he might as well chase me up the stairs to the bedrooms. Mike quickly realized what I was doing as I led Allen up the stairs. He followed behind Allen so that he wouldn't topple over backwards down the stairs.

I led Allen into his room as he held onto a fistful of the back of my shirt. I squirmed to break his hold on my shirt. When I broke loose, he swung his loosened fist at my face, but lost his balance, crashed backwards into his closet, thumping his head as he hit the floor. He was knocked-out cold. I didn't know whether he had finally passed out from the effects of the alcohol in his system or whether he knocked himself out from the whack on the head from his fall. At that point, however I was beyond compassionate caring. I just wanted to leave before he awoke and started another tirade. I gently drew a blanket over him carefully so as to not disturb him, checked to see if his breath was steady, and tip-toed down the stairs, and out the door letting him lay as he did—his head and torso in his closet and his legs extending out into the bedroom.

Chapter Nine
ACCEPTANCE OF A PROBLEM?

When I saw Allen the next day, he was quite remorseful. He knew he had been very drunk the previous night, but he didn't know how drunk. "I knew something happened last night because when I woke up this morning, I was lying in my closet with a blanket over me. Clara and Donnie were gone. Then they came home and told me that I got drunk last night, that they went over to your place, and that you and your brother were here with me."

I gave him the lengthy details about the previous evening. He couldn't remember where his truck was or where his keys were. He didn't remember much of anything, including Professor Gutierez taking him away from the tavern. Allen was astonished and embarrassed about his behavior during the early hours of the morning. When I asked him how he felt, he answered, "Fine, except for a little headache."

In spite of his remorse and embarrassment for getting plastered and violent, it was only two weeks later that he, again, came home drunk. He was not as drunk this time. He was lucid enough to be able to stop at Circle K to buy a six pack of beer on his drive home from the tavern in Independence.

Clara called me to say that Allen was drunk and that she was frightened. She asked if I would come over and sit with them for a while. Donnie was spending the night over at the house of one of his classmates and my brother Mike was working at Roth's IGA in Independence.

I walked over to their apartment with great trepidation. I arrived to find that Allen had quickly polished off four beers and was starting a fifth. I had no idea how much he had consumed prior to returning home. He was, by now, just as drunk as the time he thought I had stolen his truck, but he was fairly mellow and not at all violent. He kept pestering me to drink a beer with him. I refused. We wanted him to forget about drinking and go to bed so that we could also get some rest. As I had learned previously with Allen, the more he drank, the more alcohol he wanted.

He dipped snuff while he drank, something I was never quite sure how he did without swallowing the whole dip. Allen was a heavy snuff user, going though a tin of Copenhagen about every two days. As he sat there, drunk as Huck Finn's pa, with his glasses nearly sliding off his pug, flat nose, the residue from the Copenhagen tucked inside his lower lip dribbled out the corners of his mouth and down his chin.

To get his mind off drinking, I asked him questions about commercial fishing and fish camp. He described his boat as best as he could when he interrupted himself with a "scussme" and walked into the bathroom. Because he left the door open, Clara and I could hear the tremendous pressure all the booze he consumed at Independence had created on his bladder. To divert his attention from wanting more beer, I asked, "What do you do when you gotta piss while on you're out on the water in your boat?"

He replied with a slurred drunken chuckle, "You got the whole fucking Yukon to piss in!"

Finally much to Clara's and my relief, and after several hours of trying to convince him that he didn't need to go buy more beer, he decided to go to bed. He insisted that I sleep on his bedroom floor so he wouldn't be alone. I waited until he fell asleep, said goodnight to Clara and snuck out as quietly as I could to my own apartment.

I found Allen the next day sitting in his bedroom on his bed looking remorsefully at the broken mirror from his truck accident. He was beginning to acknowledge that he had a drinking problem and the affect it had on those around him. We tried to get at the roots of why he drank. Again, he mentioned the frustration over school and being away from his home. In truth, Allen himself didn't really know why he drank the way he did, except that he did it when he was frustrated. I kept hammering at him that he needed to realize how his drinking affected those around him. And that he needed to break out of the vicious cycle of becoming frustrated, drinking because of his frustrations, performing poorly with his studies when hung over, and getting frustrated when he performed poorly—but we had talked about this previously. And as before, I wondered if it would sink in. I could talk to him until I suffocated from lack of oxygen with no results. He had to accept his problem and want to change it.

Chapter Ten
CALLING IT QUITS

I was not able to meet the Greens at the Portland airport when they returned to Oregon after their Christmas break in Alaska. Dr. Paul Jensen met them at the airport and drove them to Monmouth instead of me. "Papa Jensen," as he was affectionately known by his Eskimo friends, was born in Denmark in 1907.

As a lad growing up in Denmark, Dr. Jensen was fascinated by tales of Arctic explorers such as Knud Rasmussen. When he was twelve years old, a group of Greenland Eskimo children attended his school in Denmark as a sort of cultural enrichment for both groups of children. Dr. Jensen, as a child then, became well acquainted with some of the children and even learned some of their native language. He maintained this interest in Arctic cultures throughout his life, eventually gaining masters and doctoral degrees from the University of North Dakota focusing on history, anthropology, and education. Even his early educational career can be considered as remarkable, for Dr. Jensen could not speak or read English when he immigrated to the United States at the age of seventeen.

In 1962, Dr. Jensen explored St. Lawrence Island located in the Bering Sea off the coast of western Alaska. He even circumnavigated the large island—246 miles around it—in an umiak, a boat roughly thirty feet long made from the skins of female walruses. Female skins were preferred because the skins of male walrus skins generally had too many scars in them to make quality umiaks.

In the decades that followed Dr. Jensen's earliest explorations in the Arctic, including a trek across the rugged Alaska Brooks Range in 1964, he made many trips to Alaska, Canada, and Greenland. Because of his keen interest and willingness to learn about indigenous Alaska cultures, Dr. Jensen gained the respect of many people, particularly those in Alaska.

While teaching Educational Psychology at Western Oregon State College (WOSC), Dr. Jensen created and implemented several programs designed to enrich the education of Alaskan Eskimo children. Early in his association with Eskimo people and schools, he became concerned that no elementary reading and language books included bilingual and bicultural enrichment for young Eskimo students, so he implemented a program to produce, print, and distribute such books to Eskimo village schools. Another program started by Dr. Jensen provided funding for education majors to spend their student teaching experience in Alaskan village schools. Remembering his childhood cultural school exchange with Greenland Eskimo children in the Danish school of his youth, Dr. Jensen started a third program which enabled Eskimo children of Alaska to attend school in Oregon. This program served a dual purpose: to provide hands-on-experience for Eskimo children in the America outside of their Alaska, and to provide Oregon children experience with Eskimo children.

Because of his extensive travels throughout Alaska, Dr. Jensen became a well known person in many rural villages. He would often talk to young people living in these villages about college. As a result, Monmouth, Oregon became a popular destination for Eskimos wanting a college education.

During the early 1980s, while Allen and I attended WOSC, Dr. Jensen and the college established the Paul Jensen Arctic Museum on campus to house his tremendous collection of Arctic artifacts, including the same female walrus-skinned umiak that he had used extensively in the 1960s and 1970s for travel off the western coast of Alaska. The museum was utilized as a research center for people all over the country studying Arctic cultures as well as an attraction for those visiting the Western Oregon State College campus. Dr. Jensen continued to work full time, managing all aspects of the museum, until he died shortly after giving a speech at the annual salmon bake fundraiser for the museum at the age of eighty-nine.

Allen and Clara had heard of Papa Jensen before they came to school at WOSC. Papa Jensen organized several potluck gatherings for the Eskimo students attending WOSC. Accordingly, Allen and Clara came to know Papa Jensen quite well so they were comfortable with Dr. Jensen to meet them at the airport in Portland.

When Allen phoned to tell me that they were back, he asked me to come over to meet someone they brought with them from Alaska. After I walked over to their apartment and welcomed them back, we waited for their "mystery person" to come out of the bathroom.

Finally, a shy Eskimo man came out. Four inches taller and perhaps twenty-five pounds lighter than Allen, he had a long bushy, thick, black mane of hair, and very thick dark-rimmed glasses. Like Allen, he also sported a black mustache, but while Allen shaved the rest of his face, this man grew his thin beard out, lending a scraggly appearance to his face.

"Hi. I'm Dan."

"I'm Clyde. I've heard a lot about you."

So this was Crazy Clyde. He spoke quietly and slowly in a halting manner like his sister Clara. I had heard of him also. He was three years older than Allen and about three years younger than Clara. He had been smoking pot habitually for nine years. He seemed almost childlike in his shyness.

Later, Allen told me privately that the folks couldn't handle Clyde's behavior anymore, that he drank almost daily. Allen and Clara brought Clyde back with them to give the folks a break from Clyde's destructiveness. I told Allen that he better find Clyde a job or get him into school to keep him busy and out of trouble. Allen agreed, and at registration, Clyde signed up for "Freshman Composition," "History of World Civilization," and a basketball class.

Clyde's presence apparently had a great influence on Allen's habits: Not that Allen drank more—quite the opposite. Perhaps Allen felt pressured to set a good example for Clyde. On Allen's twenty-eighth birthday, while studying the broken mirror again, Allen drank one beer and silently vowed to quit drinking.

The change in Allen was incredible. There were no more late-night forays to Dallas or Independence to get drunk. Allen was no longer depressed; his personality changed from being shy and awkward to one of being confident and positive. And with this upbeat approach to life, Allen's true nature emerged. He had a teasing sense of humor. People around campus began to talk about the change in him. They wanted to be around Allen, whereas previously during his drinking months, people kept their distance. His grades shot up from F's and D's to relatively easy C's and B's— even a few A's. Mutual acquaintances remarked to me that they couldn't believe the change in Allen. Clara felt extremely relieved.

The transformation in Allen did not occur overnight as it seemed to our mutual friends. Allen had nearly eighteen months of living in Monmouth, Oregon miles away from his home in Mountain Village, Alaska where drinking, drunkenness, and alcoholism touched nearly every family. Even though college towns are usually associated with wild parties and drinking, perhaps Allen felt pressured that his drinking habits exceeded the norm. On the one hand, drinking and getting drunk were considered normal and accepted weekend behaviors in a college environment. On the other hand, drinking so much, and so often, and not being able to physically handle the effects of alcohol in his body to the extent that while in drunken state, he would accost and loudly pester friends, sometimes with violence, earn a D.W.I., total his vehicle, and land in the hospital were not considered normal and accepted behaviors even in a college town. Allen was out of and away from the environment which fostered and socially permitted his particular drinking behavior and now living in a society which did not.

He had been thinking about his drinking habits for some time. Surely a D.W.I., the resulting alcohol diversion classes required of him by the state of Oregon, and a vehicle accident which totaled his first truck caused him to consider his relationship with alcohol. Also Clara, I, plus other friends badgering him to control his drinking habits forced him to think about his potential problem. For whatever reason, Allen chose to quit drinking on that night in January. Perhaps his decision was like the chronic smoker who finally gets fed up with the harmful physical and social effects of smoke and flushes the last pack down the toilet to quit cold turkey.

Like Clara, I was greatly relieved. I know it was very difficult for him. I know there were times when he craved the taste of alcohol and its numbing effects. From the first time we met, Allen and I were drawn to each other and bound together like brothers by some unexplainable force, each willing to accept the other, faults and all. A permanently sober Allen drew our friendship even closer.

Chapter Eleven
PACKING TO GO

I was frustrated with school, especially my elementary education major and wanted to change majors. I considered transferring to Oregon State University in Corvallis to major in journalism, but hadn't decided. Western Oregon State University, Monmouth, my job at the library, Allen, Clara, and others were all very important to me. They represented the stability in my life that I needed at a time when my family was splitting apart. My mother was packing to move out of the house in Silverton, Oregon. She filed for divorce from my father after twenty-three years of marriage. Perhaps someone might remark that I was searching for a new family, as I found in the Greens, when my own family disintegrated with my parents' divorce. The demise of my parents' marriage and the growth of my relationships with the Green family occurred in roughly the same period of my life.

I wasn't sure that I was up to any other big changes at this time in my life—changes in schools, communities, majors, and perhaps friends—all at once. The most important people to me were living in Monmouth.

Allen sensed my frustration. "Dan. Come to Alaska with me this summer. It is time to show you our life—our home." I agreed. It was time for me to go with him.

The upcoming spring was Clara's college graduation. Her parents, Papa Joe and Mama Arlene Green, flew from Alaska to Oregon to attend Clara's graduation. Allen and Clara's two younger sisters, Joy and MaryAnn, arrived with their parents.

The last few days before the Green family and I left for Alaska still remain as a whirlwind of fleeting images. I packed several large boxes with items I would need, checked and rechecked lists. Clara already had a teaching job lined up in the Lower Yukon School District. With the help of her mother Arlene, and sisters Joy and MaryAnn, Clara packed up all of Donnie's and her belongings to move back to Mountain Village, Alaska.

Allen and Clyde packed the items they wished to leave in Oregon for their return in the fall and stored them in a rented storage locker. I followed Allen ten miles over to Dallas, Oregon to the home of his former grade school teacher now retired after twenty years of teaching in rural Alaska. Allen intended to leave his truck with his former teacher for the summer.

Upon meeting the elder Greens, I found that, similar to meeting Clara and Allen, I liked them immediately. Arlene had a stocky build like Clara and Allen, with a warm cherubic face and twinkling eyes. She spoke English quite well slowly, but with little hesitation, or halting manner. She had a little musical lilt, a voice that was beautifully calm and warm. Arlene reassured my mother, "You don't need to worry. We'll take good care of him."

Joseph was short, older, more slightly built than his wife, and had an old man's pot-belly. His full head of steel-gray hair capped sparkling eyes that always seemed to be peering in the distance. He was very spry despite his extremely bowed legs. He communicated only in Yup'ik to his family. When speaking words to me, he spoke in a spattering of broken English words which carried larger meanings. "No big river here. Miss home. Like big river to be near." I often wish I had taken him over to the Willamette River, about five miles east of Monmouth. The Willamette seems puny when compared to the mighty Yukon. Nevertheless, the sight of another river may have soothed his homesick feelings.

Shortly after meeting Allen and Clara's parents, Allen told me, "Pop has given you an Eskimo name. Wichemaluq. It is after a very good man from our village. He was a good hunter and a very wise man. It literally means, 'was awake a long time.' This is a great honor, Dan, to be named like this. It happens very rarely. Only when one is invited and accepted into a family and a community." Years later, I reflected often on the ironic symbolism of "was awake a long time," because I have long struggled with insomnia.

At midnight, after a busy day of readying for the trip, I went to bed for a couple hours of sleep. Around 3:00 a.m. my parents came from Silverton to help everyone load up to drive to Portland. We were loaded and on the road by 4:30 a.m., traveling in a caravan of three vehicles that included all—Allen, Clara, Clyde, Donnie, Joy, and her baby—who were scheduled for the flight at 6:30 a.m. Arlene, Joseph, MaryAnn, and her baby were scheduled for a later flight.

After checking in our baggage and boxes, and finding our way to the departure gate, I shared goodbyes with my family. Up to this moment, I had seen at least one of my family members every day of my life. I had been apart from them before, but never this long. I would not see any of them for the next three months.

Allen quietly broke my thoughts. "Dan. Come. It's time to go." With that, I braced myself for the summer, looking forward to a summer of new experiences with my friend.

PART TWO
ALASKA

Chapter Twelve

THE FLIGHT

As we taxied into Seatac Airport in Seattle for a brief fifteen minute stop to board passengers bound for Anchorage, I realized that this was the last stop before Alaska. Sitting behind me, Allen must have sensed my thoughts for he jumped out of his seat, pinched my shirt, and blurted, "Dan. Come. Let's call your aunt and uncle." So we scurried out of the plane, down the ramp way and into the terminal, where we quickly found a phone.

My Aunt Maxine's and Uncle Floyd's, "Have fun and catch lots of fish," made me think that no one, other than Allen, really understood what my going to Alaska was really all about. Most seemed to think that it was a summer fishing frolic, similar to the vacations that John P. Orthodontist and his buddies take every summer when they travel to some remote fishing lodge on a "really hot secret lake." Trips such as those were frequently chronicled in outdoor magazine articles and were referred to in slang as "Me an' Joe" stories. I imagined the pictures in everyone's mind of crystal clear water lakes surrounded by jagged snowy mountain peaks and great stands of evergreen trees. Sorry folks! Not all of Alaska looks like that. Commercial fishing employs a net, not a rod and reel.

I was still too excited to sleep on the flight between Seattle and Anchorage. Being one who can seldom sit still very long, I made frequent trips to the restroom without needing to relieve myself. During one jaunt to the restroom located near the front of the plane, I noticed Donnie hanging around the flight attendant's station. Two flight attendants and one of the pilots were chattering among themselves.

Me: "Donnie—are you pestering these people?"

Donnie: (shaking his head in an exaggerated way) "Nope!"

Pilot: (to Donnie) "Boy, you're a big fella! Gonna play football someday?"

Donnie: (singsong) "Ida-no-maybe-so."

Looking at Donnie, who stood close to five feet five inches and weighed nearly 190 lbs, the pilot asked, "How old are you, son?"

"Twelve."

Donnie's voice was still childlike and had a long ways to go before it reached the cracking and foghorn qualities of most adolescent boys. Nevertheless, the pilot remarked to me loudly for Donnie's benefit, "I would have thought he was about fifteen!"

Donnie beamed ear to ear and with his fingers pushed in his pants pockets up to the knuckles as he rocked from side to side and foot to foot. All of these were typical of his actions when he was a little embarrassed and basking in the compliment from an adult. I saw these actions many times before and waited a while so as not to rush Donnie and to let him enjoy his "moment." Finally, I gently told him that we should return to our seats. One of the flight attendants said, "Yes, we'll be approaching Anchorage in twenty minutes."

Anchorage International Airport seemed like a mass of busy confusion when compared to Portland's airport which appeared so organized and business-like. People of every origin—Japanese, Japanese-Americans, Anglo-Americans, Anglo-Europeans, African Americans, as well as Native Alaskans- the Inupiats, Tlingits, Aleuts, Yup'iks, and Athabascans—all mingled together with their individual plans at one common meeting place. The airport was also undergoing construction with detours here and roped-off, boarded-up sections everywhere. Allen commented that the airport was always under construction.

After failing in our attempt to rent a car to drive around Anchorage during our five and a half hour layover, because no one in our party had both a valid driver's license and a credit card, Allen led us to a seating area that would be our "headquarters" until our departure time neared. Joy settled her little boy where he could sleep comfortably. Clara, who looked as tired as we all felt, found a chair and sat there contemplatively, perhaps to recount all that had happened in the last twenty-four hours since her graduation. Donnie waddled off towards a video game room and pop machine. Allen suggested to me that we get some fresh air.

Standing out on the observation deck overlooking the city of Anchorage with Snowy Mountain in the background, I realized for the first time that I was finally in Alaska. It was a beautiful, blue sky day with a slight crispness in the air. The three of us, Clyde, Allen, and I, watched and listened quietly. It was a time for the events of the last day to catch up with us. Clyde drew on his Marlboros. Allen offered me some Copenhagen, which I took.

Both brothers seemed to have sensed my thoughts. Clyde remarked quietly, "Dan. You're in Alaska now."

As I thought about the various implications of that statement, Allen responded, "Yes—you're in Alaska—it may not feel like Alaska yet, here in Anchorage, but wait till we're at Fish Camp."

I tried to imagine what Fish Camp looked like and couldn't. Even though we were only in Anchorage, I could still feel a difference in the energy in the air, a different feeling from being in the "Lower Forty-Eight."

"Have you seen Clyde?"

"No?!"

We were standing in line to check in our tickets. It was five minutes to four and our flight to St. Mary's was scheduled to leave on the hour. After Clara remarked that she had seen Clyde in the lounge, I remembered seeing him in the restroom. He disappeared shortly after we returned to our "headquarters" in the airport and after our visit to the observation deck.

Allen dashed off in the direction of the lounge. Not long after we boarded the little plane, within a few minutes, Allen scrambled into the plane. After catching his breath, he said he couldn't find Clyde so Allen had his brother paged.

The plane was a Beechcraft turbo-prop, very small with only ten passenger seats. With the absence of Clyde, there were only seven in our group. Two strangers—"kass'aqs"—sat in the two seats closest to the pilot. I wondered why they were flying to St. Mary's, Alaska, our flight destination.

In those quick minutes, we all wondered where Clyde was and if he would make it to the flight. We had various theories for the reason for his absence. Clara spoke matronly of her younger brother in her slow deliberate way: "Clyde's old enough to be responsible for himself. But he always does these things to make us worry."

Allen responded, "He probably didn't want to leave today," with a shrug of his shoulders.

"Where will he stay tonight?" I asked.

"Oh, he'll probably stay at the airport tonight and catch a flight tomorrow if there is one. Or he'll call one of his friends here in Anchorage to stay the night."

We all knew that meant if Clyde was dead-drunk now, he could be in worse shape by tomorrow.

It was 4:05 and the pilot couldn't wait any longer, so we left Anchorage without Clyde. I had chosen a seat near the back of the plane, right next to the door through which we had boarded. I later regretted my choice in seating because the door apparently had an air leak in the sealing around it, and the air whistled in my left ear the whole three-and-a-half-hour flight to St. Mary's. I plucked my old wool navy-blue stocking cap out of my backpack and pulled it down tightly over my chilled balding head.

Allen sat across the narrow aisle from me and fiddled around with his camera. Clara was in the seat directly in front of him and sat crossways with her feet in the aisle with her back against the window. She looked at me with a loving glow on her face.

"Danny Boy." No one ever called me that, except my father.

Allen looked up from what he was doing, toward Clara, and then at me. He smiled, and with the same loving glow on his face as his sister, he repeated teasingly, "Danny Boy."

It was their chance to show me their home. I looked after them in Oregon and now they would look after me. I relaxed, and then looked back and forth at the two rounded faces I had grown to love. I hadn't realized how tense I was with all the excitement and anticipation building up but Clara must have sensed it. I was always amazed as to how sensitive she and Allen were about people. They were gifted with a sixth sense because they were often able to know what people are thinking or feeling, yet, neither Clara nor Allen were aware of this gift. It was just there. Perhaps it is a part of people whose culture relies mostly on visual observation as a primary means of learning. I wondered if Clara had intended to make me feel calm. It was certainly working.

The three-and-a-half hour flight to St. Mary's in our light craft was very rough. Sometimes we experienced turbulence so rough that I could hear the plywood box which held the small cast-iron stove that Allen purchased at G.I. Joes in Oregon, jump a little. Turning around to look behind me, I could see it sitting there in the freight compartment separated from the passenger compartment by a very heavy gauge cable. While looking at it, I remembered watching the plane being loaded with our freight from a freight transport back at the Anchorage airport. Clara had the most baggage and boxes since she and Donnie were moving back to Alaska from Oregon to begin a career in teaching. I had the second largest amount of freight consisting of two large cardboard boxes, which held my sleeping bag, pillow, parka, rain clothes, toiletries, other miscellaneous items and a large green army-type duffle bag which contained my other clothes. Allen hadn't brought much since he put his school materials, clothes, bedding, and kitchen items into a mini-storage rental unit and all of his fishing/camping/outdoor gear was already in Alaska. The others had come to Oregon to witness Clara's graduation, so each only had small suitcases.

Finally, the two men loading the small plane reached what we had been jokingly anticipating—the stove. Hidden in its homemade plywood box, which Allen and his dad constructed in Oregon out of scrap lumber, it looked quite small and unobtrusive sitting on the flatbed of the freight transport truck next to Clara's and my large boxes.

One of the men grabbed the two rope handles on the sides of the homemade plywood box holding the cast-iron stove with gusto. We could almost hear him groan and curse even at our distance with wind and windows separating us. The other man hastened over to help and the two struggled to shuffle the box over to the plane. They couldn't lift it up onto the edge of the luggage compartment floor which was about level with their chins. While we chuckled at their plight, a third man ran over to help, and together the three succeeded. I felt a little guilty for laughing at the scene and wondered if one of them had acquired a hernia with his efforts.

We flew over the Alaska Range, miles and miles of the most rugged, jagged mountains that could possibly have existed anywhere. Finally, the mountains gave way to a wild, barren-looking, rolling plain. The tundra. Water was everywhere. Lakes, streams, sloughs, and bogs laced and dotted the tundra so that one could not decide where the main river of the mighty Yukon River really was.

It is incomprehensible how isolated "civilization" is in the Lower Yukon Delta region—miles and miles of total vastness, rolling hills of tundra and water. Nothing else. It seemed so empty. Yet this region just teems with wildlife and is the breeding grounds of some of the highest concentrations of waterfowl in the world.

As we passed over a tiny Eskimo village, Clara and Allen argued whether it was Holy Cross or Russian Mission. I thought, "God—we're almost there." The names and places that they had been talking about for the last two years were becoming a reality.

We came descending into this wild, watery landscape with a menagerie of exploited senses and thoughts. Most of us were ill from the rough flight. Donnie vomited on the floor of the plane. Joy's baby bawled while further soiling his already dirty pants. Allen's snuff juices dribbled down his chin, and Clara spit sunflower seed husks onto the floor. The odor in the small confines of the rocky cabin of the little plane combined with the effect of total exhaustion was overwhelmingly nauseating. As we started our slow, bumpy descent to a tiny dot of civilization on the lower Yukon River, St. Mary's, I felt like an alien might feel when entering into an unknown world.

Allen's oldest brother, Leonard, and Joy's boyfriend, Tim, father of their baby, met us at the airport. Leonard was about my height (tall for a Yup'ik Eskimo) and much heavier. He closely resembled his mother, had much less nervous energy and quieter than Allen. He was more like Clyde than Allen in disposition.

The eighteen-mile gravel road was the only "highway" in the whole region runs parallel to the Yukon between the villages of St. Mary's and Mountain Village. The drive between these two communities takes about one and a half hours to drive one way, so I was told.

Still a bit edgy from the flight, I rode with Tim, Joy, and their baby in his dented, rusted wreck of a tiny 1981 Ford Courier pickup. We were followed by Leonard, Allen, Clara, and the rest, all of whom rode in the cab and bed of Joseph Green's full-size, four-wheel-drive Ford pickup truck.

The springs in the seat of the Ford Courier were bouncy, and being taller than the average Yup'ik Eskimo male, I repeatedly clubbed my head on the roof of the small pickup cab with the worst bumps, much to the humor of Tim, our driver, who was about my age and known to beat his common-law wife on a regular drinking schedule. Joy sat between us clutching their shitting, spitting, bawling baby and told of how well-behaved the boy had been on the trip.

I felt for the boy, knowing full well that he faced a life of desperation which was poverty surrounded by alcohol abuse and a world of tremendous change. Tim must have been quite attached to the little fellow for when the boy quieted, he insisted on holding him in one arm while driving with the other. I had to admire the child because I didn't think I would be quiet very long if I had sticky poop in my pants! The boy seemed to be the only bond between Joy and Tim; the only thing they seemed to have in common was their love for their shared offspring.

While pondering at the boy's future, I looked out the window of the pickup and gripped the make-shift rope door handle to keep the door closed. I found myself scanning the miles of tundra in hopes of seeing a single substantial tree. Suddenly I became aware of the extreme isolation and culture shock I was experiencing. I thought of Allen and Clara, Yup'ik Eskimos and close friends riding in the truck behind us who brought them to Alaska to fish with them and live with their family in their culture. I marveled at the strength of their people to have carved a life out of this unforgiving region and who, for a millennium, loved it and called it home.

More thoughts flooded into my head, and I wondered if Allen and Clara felt, as I felt now, when leaving their home to go to college in Oregon. Oregon with all of its trees, hills, people and rainy, cloudy, depressing winters seemed uncomfortably distant. I thought about the stay in rural-Eskimo Alaska ahead of me, how it would change me, how much I would learn, and how I might feel when I finally returned home.

Chapter Thirteen
MOUNTAIN VILLAGE

Mountain Village is a large Eskimo settlement of 800 people scattered near the base of a very large hill. The older section of the community consisted of homes that were no more than tiny shacks, the Catholic Church, village school, post office, village store, and village cannery all aligned along the Yukon. The developing, newer section grew up the smaller hills away from the river and toward the road that leads into town from St. Mary's.

The road running between St. Mary's and Mountain Village was the only road in this whole region. There were, of course, "streets" in the two communities; these "streets" were constructed of gravel, dirt and rocks. There was no road leaving St. Mary's in the opposite direction upriver toward the community of Pilot Station, nor was there any road leaving Mountain Village downriver in the direction of the Bering Sea. Moreover, most communities in this Lower Yukon River Delta Region did not have any roads connecting them at all. Their only access to a world beyond their community was by boat on the river in the summer. In the winter snow machines, cars or pickup trucks traveled up and down the iced-over river. Airplanes were the only means of transportation available for all seasons, but even then, these were highly dependent on quality flying conditions. Great barges crept up the river from the Bering Sea in the summer, bringing supplies and fuel for houses and engines, food, and other basic staples, even a vehicle or two.

Most of the newer homes in the community were built in the late 1970s and were all built with the same basic floor plan—with blue corrugated metal roofs and dark brown or beige-colored wood siding. They all sat high on concrete blocks raising them about five feet above the tundra. Often there was a small doorway

Older houses along the Yukon River at Mountain Village, Alaska.

in these foundation walls indicating that the five foot high space between the ground and the floor of the house could be used for storage. I discovered later that some people stored their ATVs and snow machines in these spaces.

Joseph Green's home was one of the newer houses. Allen said that even though they had lived there for several years and had much more room than in their old house by the river, where Leonard lived alone, they still were not used to the new house. It was about three-quarters of a mile from the river. Papa Joseph explained to me later in his beautifully simple English, "Too far from Yukon." I knew what he meant as he was born on the banks of the Yukon, had spent his entire life living along and on the river as it provided his whole means of life. The Yukon was his life-blood. It flowed richly through his veins and I could see it clearly in his black, old eyes. He wanted to be close enough to see, hear, smell, feel, and live the river all the time.

Mom and Pop Green's visit to Oregon for Clara's graduation was the first time in their lives they had been "outside." When they were asked how they liked Oregon, Ma, who was always the most vocal of the two exclaimed with a big smile and gentle singing voice, "So pretty. And so warm and there's no mosquitoes." Joseph stated flatly, "No big river."

To enter into these homes, one had to get through two doors. The first door, the outside one, was reached after climbing seven or eight steps to a landing surrounded by a railing making it handy for the tobacco chewers and smokers to lean on while shooting the breeze and wishing to complete their habits in the fresh air.

Just inside the outside door was a room affectionately referred to as "the mud room." This small room approximately eight-feet-by-eight-feet was where everyone intending to enter into the main part of the house was expected to remove dirty, muddy articles of clothing, especially footwear. In one corner of the mud room of most of these homes sat a small stack of split and ready to burn firewood for the wood stove which is auxiliary heating for these homes. On top of the stack of wood, typically was the entree for tonight or tomorrow's supper- usually fish, beaver, a hunk of moose, or a carcass of a waterfowl.

Next to the wood stack, in some of these homes, leaned a well-used chainsaw and a battered axe. There may be a couple of five gallon plastic buckets referred to as honey buckets. Many Eskimo villages had modern sewer and water system consisting of sinks with hot and cold running water, and flush toilets, but often the community's water and sewer system is shut down for repairs. During these times, one went into the mud room and used the honey bucket as a temporary toilet.

After being impressed with the nifty and very useful mudroom, I followed Allen through the second door— the one entering the main part of the house. I was surprised to discover that there were four bedrooms in this little house. Small though they were, the bedrooms were very functional with a single bed, a small closet, and a small window.

Allen's bedroom was the one closest to the entrance door; the bedroom next to it was designated as mine. MaryAnn and her two-year-old daughter, Lucy, had the room in the furthest corner of the house because they had a double bed and a couple of dressers. Mom and Pop had the bedroom down the hall from MaryAnn's. On the other side at the end of the second hallway, near the folks' room, was the bathroom. The folks had a single-twin mattress on the floor of their room; that is what they both slept on. I noticed that Allen's bed did not have a mattress on it, only a long piece of corrugated cardboard on top of the bare spring frame of the bed. He slept with only the cardboard separating him from the bare, cold poking springs. It didn't take much mental geometry to figure out that MaryAnn had the parents' double bed, probably because she had Lucy, and the folks were using Allen's mattress on the floor of their bedroom.

I asked where Clyde would be sleeping and wondered when he would finally make it home. I wanted to know if I were taking his room. Allen replied "No," most of Clyde's belongings were in the old house where Leonard lived down by the river and that Clyde often slept there. He further added that when Clyde was at the folk's house, he usually slept out on the hide-a-bed couch in the living room because he usually was the last one in at night. A quick glance at Allen's face told me that Clyde was not sober when he came home on those late nights.

Clara had her own two-bedroom house similar in style as the folks' house, but she was scared to stay there alone with just Donnie—afraid a drunk might try to break in while she was still there. Clara slept somewhere in MaryAnn's room, whether in the double bed with MaryAnn and Lucy or on the floor, I couldn't be certain. That room was off limits to the adult males living in the house. Donnie slept down at the old house along the Yukon with Leonard, his favorite uncle.

After we dropped off our luggage, we walked up the road to the house of another sister of Allen and Clara's; apparently she was making dinner for all of the arrivals. We stopped first at Clara's house to see how it weathered the winter while she was away at college. The door was still closed and locked, but was loose on both sides, evidence that some force had put considerable pressure on the door—not enough to break it in, but enough to loosen the screws in the wood of the door's hinges and door clasp. When Clara unlocked and opened the door, we saw a crack in the door frame running up from the door latch-hole and continued downward from it to the bottom of the frame. Clara had a look of genuine fear on her face and exclaimed, "Oh-no!"

Looking at the door and back at her, I had the slow realization of the terrible grip that alcohol had on the community. No sober Eskimo would have tried to break in her door especially not in a village where everybody knew everybody and most were related. Only a drunk or other crazed individual would do this, someone looking for more booze money.

Ellen's house was right across the road from Clara's and was the home farthest away from the river, the last in the growth of the village up along the St. Mary's road. Her house was the same model as Clara's and the folks'. None of the homes I visited while in Alaska had carpeted floors, except that of Phillip, who is Allen and Clara's other college-educated sibling. His home was one of the nicest in Mountain Village. In most of the houses, the bare wood floors looked like they were huge panels of OSB board covered with a light varnish. The inside walls of the houses appeared to be made of the same material as the floors.

After a hearty meal of roast beaver and boiled herring eggs on seaweed, the latter procured from some relatives living on the coast of the Bering Sea, and relaying the details of our trip and the school year in Oregon to pregnant Ellen, Allen, Clara, and I walked down through town. Ellen's five-year-old daughter, IdaMae, a delightful little four-year-old girl, tagged along with us. The village is a hilly and rocky trek with little kids constantly cruising around on ATVs. Evidence of the destruction of alcohol was almost everywhere. Nearly every pickup truck, a common vehicle here, suffered the incapacities of a boozy, errant driver. No truck seemed immune from bodily injury with bashed-in truck beds, broken windows, smashed grills, and a barrage of dents.

As we neared the river, we turned on a road that paralleled it. The road led out of town to where it would end after two miles at the village dump. In the middle of the steep bank between the road and the river was a wide shelf on which perched the oldest homes in the community. Most of these older homes were no more than simple shacks separating the inhabitants from the harsh climate. Even the better-built of these older homes were so small when compared to our "Lower Forty-eight" standards that it was hard to imagine the typical large Eskimo family of eight to twelve members living in one.

Allen and Clara were born in one of the sturdier built houses. No one lived in it now; the Green family used it for storage. It had a large mudroom where two large chest freezers were kept. The main part of the house had only three rooms: a large combination room for kitchen and living area, and two smaller rooms. It was obvious that both Clara and Allen had fond memories of their first home for they both had slight smiles and wistful dreamy looks as their eyes wandered over the room bare of anything except a rack of moose antlers Allen had harvested the year before. Clara startled me by saying, "Dan. You live here someday!"

I looked at both of their gentle faces and their loving, gripping eyes. Several thoughts jumbled around in my head searching for a response appropriate for the moment. Whenever Clara, Allen, or even Donnie spoke to me, they always began with an emphatic "Dan" followed by a long pause before beginning their statement or question. I glanced around the room quickly but not hurriedly, wondering what it would be like to live in this little house with no running water. Clara was telling me that this could be my house someday while showing me that she was welcoming me to Alaska, yet I wasn't even sure how I felt about Yup'ik Eskimo Alaska, or whether I would ever want to come back here again after this summer, to live or to visit. Of course, it was way too soon to be making any such decisions.

I looked back at their glowing, expectant faces and the only thing I could say for the anticipated response was "Yah," and attempt to return their radiant expression.

We left the uninhabited little house and walked next door to the second and slightly larger home of Joseph and Arlene, the one they had lived in before moving into the "new house" house. Allen and Clara's oldest brother Leonard lived here. We were silently gazing over the immense Yukon while the wind blew incessantly. Their black hair flowed free; mine lay trapped under my cap.

Allen said, "Tomorrow, we'll put the boat down."

While I contemplated what all "putting the boat down" might involve, Clara said, "Allen, maybe you can take us to pick rhubarbs."

Allen replied smiling and patting me on the shoulder, "Yeh, Dan's first boat ride."

We turned to the "new house' very tired after not having slept for forty hours. With cog-wheels spinning at a hundred RPMs in our minds, we went to bed and slept right through all of the late night phone calls. Only Allen, Clara, Ellen's daughter, IdaMae, and I stayed in the house that night. It was the quietest night spent in Mountain Village all summer.

Chapter Fourteen
THE BOAT

After a hearty breakfast of oatmeal laced with raisins, Allen and I set off toward the river to one of the "old houses," which now was Leonard's house, to "put the boat down." It was about 11:30 a.m. The town's daily activities were just winding up. Typically, with the long sunshine Alaskan days, most people, including us, got into the habit of going to bed around 2:00 or 3:00 a.m. and rising around 10:00 or 11:00 a.m.

As we walked through town, I couldn't help but feel a little uncomfortable from the stares we were receiving. Allen explained that the only other white people in town during the summers were the family that ran the village store and the priest. But in the winter months, the priest and a few teachers at the school were the only Caucasians seen around the village. A few vagabond kuss'aqs (the word Yup'iks call whites) straggled in and out of town. These few men, usually bootleggers or dope peddlers, were the major reason for disharmony between the whites and Yup'iks. These men exploited and took from the Eskimos leaving little in return other than destruction. Men of these types were often the first contact with white men that Eskimos had after Catholic missionaries filtered into Alaska after Vitas Bering's explorations of the western coast of Alaska in 1741 (Morgan 34).

In the latter part of the 1700s up to 1867, when the United States purchased Alaska from Russia, many Russian traders and trappers arrived in southwestern Alaska and with them alcohol and disease. The influence of these first Russian men is still present even in the names of some of the communities, such as "Russian Mission." Many Russian words have become part of the Yup'ik language. For example, a Russian word for a group of Russian people noted for their

Older houses along the Yukon River at Mountain Village, Alaska.

horsemanship is "Cossack" and the Yup'iks use the term, "kuss'aqs," to refer to white people.

The Catholic influence is also very strong in southwest Alaska. Saint Mary's and Holy Cross are official modern names of Yup'ik Eskimo villages. The community of St. Mary's, fifteen miles up river from Mountain Village, is named after the Catholic mission, school, and church that reside in the community.

Although most of the Yup'ik Eskimos I came into contact with were friendly, if not a little shy and reserved, the old tensions between Eskimos and white continue to exist. The sale of alcohol is prohibited by village law in most of these Alaskan communities, including Mountain Village. However, booze is readily available, flown in illegally from Anchorage by bootleggers and distributed somewhat discreetly at exorbitant prices such as $60 per pint of whiskey.

One day after I had been in Alaska for several weeks and had somewhat recovered from culture shock and the "newness" of Alaska, I was walking through town from the old house by the river to the new house, when I heard a drunken question, apparently directed at me. Allen had forbade me to walk around the village alone, but on that day, I needed some alone-time.

"Hey! White Man! What are you doing here?"

I stopped walking, my heart pounding in my chest. I looked over at the inebriated speaker, a Yup'ik male of about thirty-five years old. I wondered if he were speaking to me specifically or he was philosophically asking a general question referring to the race of Caucasians. Perhaps the hazy image of me had triggered him to speak his reflected thought aloud, echoing a general question on most Yup'iks' minds since the first presence of white men in the land.

Stalling for time to think and not wanting to make my fears of the moment known, I walked deliberately over to the sagging porch where the man was leaning. Would he attempt to swing a bicycle at me as I had seen others do when drunk and angry?

"What did you say?"

"Who are you and what are you doing here?"

Although he was obviously "under the influence," he was not as intoxicated as I had first thought. I answered him by smiling and extending my hand to greet his.

"My name is Dan. I'm a classmate of Allen Green. We go to college together down in Oregon. He asked me to come up and work with him this summer."

"Oh. I heard Clara graduated and thought you a husband she brought home."

I broke out laughing, "No. Clara's my friend also. But she is about twelve years older than me." To this he laughed and seemed satisfied that I was not the devil reincarnated. We talked of fishing for a while and then broke company. He invited me to come visit him again.

As Allen and I completed our mile and a half trek through town to the Yukon to "put the boat down," I noticed a Ford Bronco parked in front of the older Green house. It had a bashed-in right front fender, broken right mirror; the calamities continued with a spider-webbing of cracks in the right side of the front window.

"Whose truck?"

"Leonard's. Got drunk one night and caused some trouble. He has to spend some time in St. Mary's jail for his fine. Do you see that yellow Ski-Doo? Clyde's. He bought it brand new last fall. Got drunk and ran into a power pole last winter. Totaled it. He was lucky he didn't get hurt."

About two weeks later, when we were down at Leonard's house getting ready to go out on the river, I was sitting outside with Clyde watching the gulls which were swooping around and croaking their raucous song. I motioned to the wreckage of the yellow Ski-Doo snowmobile and asked Clyde, "Whose is that?"

After a pause, Clyde cleared his throat and said, "Uh, I, uh-ah, found it last winter near St. Mary's and towed it back for parts. Uh—ah—somebody must have got drunk and wrecked it."

Allen and I continued on our "putting the boat down" project. We scrambled down the steep bank of the Yukon to where his boat lay upside down among some weeds. He stored it there last August before going down to Oregon to attend school. Allen and his father built it six summers before. It was a twenty-two foot long, all wooden, flat bottomed craft. The boat was painted every spring before the fishing season began; Allen paid his oldest nephew, Zach, to do the job, since he was in Oregon and unable to do it himself.

I realized now what "putting the boat down" meant. Somehow we had to drag, carry, push, or pull this heavy thing down to the water and turn it over. Phase two of the operation was getting the two motors down to the boat down the bank to the water. The smaller "kicker," a fifteen-horse powered Johnson, would be no problem because it really wasn't very heavy. Still, carrying anything up or down a steep bank that slanted at a seventy-five degree angle was very sporting, especially considering the unavailability of a firm stable footing among the debris, weeds, and mud. Allen's fifty-horse powered Evinrude was going to be another story, as it was much heavier than the much smaller Johnson. Then it dawned on me that Allen, his brothers, and father faced this task every spring. And every fall, there awaited the task of getting the boat and motors back up the bank for winter. I surmised that there had to be an easier, less dangerous way of doing it.

The two of us carefully grunted the boat over onto its bottom revealing the inside of the boat which looked like any typical twelve to fifteen foot basic rod and reel sport fishing boat—just longer and wider—and made of wood rather than aluminum. It had two butt-board plank seats, one near the bow and one at the stern. Then Allen located a particular piece of plywood that fit neatly in the boat covering the floor space between the two seats. The plywood would provide a smooth surface to support supplies for traveling to fish camp and would also support the fish-catch-tote which would be used during commercial fishing hours.

Allen said, "We're going to need some help getting the boat down to the water." I thought that was an understatement.

He motioned to two young men working outside of a shack standing roughly seventy-five yards away from Leonard's house. "Maybe they can help us."

The two brothers were cousins of Allen's from Pilot Station, Ivan and Sam Green, twenty-six and sixteen years old who came up to Mountain Village each spring to fish. The shack they slept in had no running water and no electricity. Except for typical fishing clothing and gear, the shack was very bare containing only two army cots, two well used sleeping bags, a wind-up alarm clock, and very few cooking and eating utensils.

Sam offered something to drink, "Water?"

Allen: "Thanks."

They chatted in Yup'ik for a short while. I had been looking for some hefty and strong boat–moving help, like Allen, but these two men were small and slightly built. Ivan, the younger and smaller, couldn't have weighed more than 120 pounds and had a persistently deep cough, after which he spit green chunks out the open door of the shack. I was sure he had pneumonia...or something else. While Sam and Allen chattered on, I asked Ivan, "Have you seen a nurse?"

"What for?"

"Your cough. I had pneumonia three years ago and coughed just like that."

"Oh—it's just a little cold, I think. Sometimes it's better, sometimes worse."

I looked at sixteen-year-old Ivan, watched him push his battered glasses up his nose repeatedly. They were wire frames that were missing the plastic nose pads. His "sometimes worse—sometimes better" sounded more like an old man discussing his ailment rather than a teenager.

Ivan struggled a can of Copenhagen out of his back pocket and opened it. I had seen Allen and others perform this act countless times. Yet instead of the typical pinch of fingers and thumb, and placing of the dip between cheek and gum, Ivan licked the surface of the snuff in the can with his sickly tongue to gain a dip. Then he offered some to me. I politely declined.

Soon we were back to our task. "Pick-it-up. Don't let it drag. I don't want the bottom to get scraped up," Allen snapped as the four of us stumbled the Titanic down the bank. We let it stay half-way out of the water so it wouldn't drift away.

I don't know how much a fifty-horse Evinrude kicker weighs, but I do know they are very heavy. It would have been nice if each of us could have had two strong handholds when carrying the kicker down the bank, but because of the treacherously sheer steep bank with poor footing, it was just too hard to get eight hands in lift-aiding places. Two strong men could have carried the kicker on a flat, even surface, but that was impossible on this steep, rugged river bank. Allen was just about as strong as any two of the rest of us, and since he was the owner of the kicker, he did most the work.

Chapter Fifteen
BOOZE AND RHUBARBS

After "getting the boat down," changing the oil in the kickers, lubing them, and mounting them on the boat, Allen and I headed back towards the new house for lunch. When we arrived, we found that someone had picked up the folks, Clyde, and MaryAnn from their flight into St. Mary's and brought them to the house. The noise level in the house had changed considerably from the previous quiet. Donnie was now teasing his two-year old cousin, Lucy, causing her to fuss and scream.

While the folks unpacked in their bedroom, the rest of us watched TV in the front room. We heard the outside door open and close; then, a few shuffled steps out in the mudroom. The inside door opened and in burst a loud and very drunk Yup'ik man carrying a brown paper sack.

"Juscumtoseeifenybudy's home."

The room quickly became very quiet except for the chatter of the TV. Little IdaMae crawled slowly onto my lap. Allen greeted the man pleasantly yet guardedly, "Pete, how are you?"

"'m drunk. Eskimoalwaysdrunk. No good. Alcoholmakeyoubad. I'm drunk."

A long period of reflective silence passed finally breaking with Allen offering him a seat to which Pete replied loudly again, "I'm drunk. Alcohol no good for Eskimo. This bag had a bottle full of booze. Now mostly empty. Here...Leonard." He fished in the bag, found the bottle that still contained liquid and tossed it to Leonard.

Leonard opened the bottle, drained its remaining contents in one breath, capped it while smacking his lips—"Aaaahh," opened the window and tossed the bottle out with an aura of macho gusto. Leonard's bit part of the scene lasted

Exploring a clear water stream that drains into the lower Yukon River. The Yukon River water has a lot of silt in it. Waters draining into the Yukon are much cleaner.

perhaps ten seconds and was executed in a fluid motion and enacted so impulsively with no thought of any possible consequences that I wondered what else Leonard did impulsively.

Pete laughed drunkenly, teetering a bit on his feet and repeated his "I'm drunk," line. Allen suggested that he should go home to sleep and gently shepherded him towards the door.

"Sleep! Yah, that's good. I go sleep now."

Clara and MaryAnn pestered Allen for a boat ride so that they could check wild rhubarbs to see if they were ready to eat.

During my first boat ride, as Allen and Clara called it, my mind was filled with an assortment of thoughts. My previous experiences with boats and water could be totaled on one hand, including a raft made out of empty plastic milk-gallon-jugs in Aberdeen, South Dakota where I spent my youth. That particular vessel never had a true floatation test because during the drought-stricken summer when we constructed it, Moccasin Creek had a water depth of four inches and a gumbo-mud depth of two feet. Almost anyone other than me would have brought better experience to a job that involved boating and commercial fishing on a very large rugged river.

I was very nervous and yet wonderfully excited as the wind pressed against our faces, streaming the hair back from everyone's foreheads. When the boat hit a rift of waves, spray flew into our faces making the bit of anxiety in me fade to be replaced by eager anticipation. Every Yup'ik face in the boat was grinning as if to express this was the best part of living—to be on the river going to pick wild rhubarbs on a warm sunny day.

Allen slowed the boat as we approached a net set in the water near the shore between two stakes. Sometimes one end of the net would be anchored on the shore with the other end staked somewhere out in the water. When MaryAnn suggested we check the net, Allen maneuvered the boat along side carefully so that his kicker blades were kept a safe distance from the net. As the kicker idled slowly, Clyde stood and shuffled carefully to the edge of the boat to lean over and grasp the net.

I stood up nervously, remembering my mother's warning "never stand up in a boat" and her repeated rendering of the time when she and Dad tipped a canoe over on their honeymoon. But this was no canoe. You had to stand up to pull in the net when fishing, yet standing there with my quaky land-lubber legs trying to get used to the gentle rhythm of the waves rocking the boat, I wondered if I would ever get used to being a riverman. I felt like the greenest of greenhorns. I turned my head awkwardly to see if Allen was watching me.

"Bend your knees, Dan. Make yourself looser. You'll get used to it. We spend a lot of time on the river in summer. Maybe even more time than you spend in your car. Weather gets much, much rougher than this. This…(he motioned with his hands)…almost calm."

Clyde pulled in one fish. Together, he and Allen attempted to explain how the markings on this one, a chum, or "dog-salmon" as most Eskimos called them, differed from a king salmon. The major difference is in the spots appearing on the upper part of the king salmon and the lack of such spots on the "dogs." King salmon, also known as "Chinook," is just that, the "king" in both size and richness of flavor. Yup'ik Eskimos preferred to eat king salmon far more than the chum which they regularly fed to their dogs when there was a surplus during subsistence fishing—hence the nickname for chum salmon—"dog salmon."

After Clyde dropped the fish in the boat and released the net, Allen eased the boat slowly away, and then opened the throttle wide to speed us toward the rhubarb upriver. All this time, I had been wondering about rhubarb. The only kind of rhubarb that I was familiar with was the low, huge-leafed plant that was commonly used for baking pies; rhubarb pie was one of Grandma Syljuberget's specialties. Allen cut the throttle to coast into a very small cove from which rose a steep bank. Clyde leapt out of the boat and held its bow while the rest of us maneuvered ourselves out and onto the shore. We set down our unworn jackets and plastic bags which eventually would contain the harvested rhubarb. Clyde and Clara grasped one side of the bow with MaryAnn and Allen on the other. They looked like they meant to pull the boat up further, so trying to be helpful, I leapt to assist them on Clyde and Clara's side. Allen grunted, "Lift, Dan. I don't want the bottom scraped." This was the second time Allen had said this in the past two days. I would hear it often throughout the course of the summer.

These rhubarbs were about the same height as the ones in Grandma Syljuberget's garden but with much smaller leaves. If left to grow to seed in the short Alaska growing season, some of the plants could grow to over three feet tall with small rhubarb leaves bowing out from the stalk. The stalk, however, with its woody, alternating wine-red and pale green appearance, most closely resembled the rhubarb with which I was familiar.

I was shown how to pull them out of the tundra, to peel the first layer on the root up to where it joins the stalk. They munch on the root area much like you would a carrot. Although a bit tart, they nevertheless were much sweeter than varieties of raw rhubarb I had eaten previously. We all ate samples of the roots before gathering some for the freezer to use later in baking and for salads.

As we sat on the tundra bank, watching the wide Yukon surge by, and listening to the droning of a distant kicker motor, my tensions, which had been building up from the previous week, continued to dissolve. It seemed like an idyllic life, sitting in the mild Yukon sun pulling and eating rhubarbs.

Chapter Sixteen
FISH CAMP

Anxious to get down the river to see his fish camp after being away in Oregon for ten months, Allen cracked a whip the next morning to get everything ready for the trip. Only Mike, Allen, and I would be going, the first to see the condition of the camp after a long winter. I decided to take everything I would need for the summer with us to camp, leaving only a blanket and a change of clothes behind at the house for those times that we would be sleeping over at Mountain Village. I expected that we would be spending most of the summer at fish camp.

Allen's older sister, Ellen, had previously cohabitated with a white man for several years and their union produced four children: Jimmy, eleven-years-old; Mike, seven-years old; Ida Mae, four-years-old; and Lizzy, three-years old. The white man deserted the family shortly after Lizzy was born. Ellen was now living with an Inuit man from Nome, Irvin, and was pregnant with his child. The little girls, Ida Mae and Lizzy, stayed with their mother, Ellen, and her new man, Irvin.

Mike and Jimmy attached themselves to their favorite uncle, just as fatherless Donnie had attached himself to Leonard. I couldn't decide whether the boys just attached themselves to a certain uncle or whether the man just took charge of a boy. Whatever the case, there were three uncle-nephew units in the Green family that worked like a father-son relationship, and each person in each unit appeared to benefit from the relationship. The fatherless boys gained father-type role model figures who taught the boys how to hunt, fish, handle a boat, and snow machine, and many other traditional tasks that young Yup'ik boys must learn to become productive capable riverine adults.

The uncles, in turn, gained a son by the nephews and nearly achieved hero-worship status from the admiring boys. Indeed it was not uncommon to hear the

Two sets of brothers. Uncles and nephews. The boys are sons of a sister of the two men. On lunch break from constructing a cabin tent.

boys trying to out-brag each other on the virtues and accomplishments of their favorite uncles. One could often hear young Mike's piping voice, "Allen did..." followed by Donnie's booming forceful, "Well, Leonard did..." and Jimmy adding a low, gentle, "Phillip did..."

After the pickup truck ride down to the old house on the shore, loading the boat, and traveling the short water distance upriver to the village store to fill gasoline barrels, we were finally at our last stop before heading downriver to a natural spring where we filled our drinking water jugs. Someone long ago had strategically placed a pipe to funnel the majority of the trickle into a single stream thus making it easy to fill buckets. The residents of Mountain Village filled their containers with this natural spring water to use for drinking and cooking at their summer fish camps.

Allen informed me that the water had been tested several years before and was found nearly pure and fit for human consumption. Almost like a salesman, he kept extolling the virtues of their "cleanest, best tasting water." I wondered what impurities may have gotten into the water system since "several years ago" and was curious about just how long a period of time Allen was talking about when he said, "several years ago." But Allen was right; the water did taste better and purer than any I had tasted before.

When Allen managed to coax the boat to its maximum traveling speed, and we were at last zooming downriver towards fish camp, I was again overwhelmed by the extreme isolation. At least in the back country of Oregon, you knew that there would be some civilization in almost any direction even if many miles stretched between you and it. Here, however, you could feel somehow that there was civilization either the direction downriver way beyond fish camp or upriver beginning with Mountain Village. But if you looked to either side, to either shore and beyond, you realized that no hint of civilization could be found for as far as one could travel across the miles and miles of rolling, mushy, marshy, vast tundra with its teeming wildlife.

When we approached a fork in the river around the island, Allen steered into the smaller right channel where the water was considerably calmer than the whitecaps on the left and main channel. After cruising along the side of the island for about thirty to forty-five minutes, we shot past the end and joined the main channel of the Yukon.

Upon leaving the smaller channel to join the main Yukon, we found ourselves on the right hand side of the river. The Green family fish camp lies on the other side of the river on another long, skinny island. Allen knew the best place to cross the river to get to camp in the shortest time. Halfway across the wide river, I finally spotted three radio towers. Allen stated that the towers marked the camp and were used for CB radio communication with other families that camped up and down the river.

Allen and I jumped out of the boat into shallow water near the shore where the boat grounded. As we stood in the eight inches of cold water, sand, and muck, a vital reason for always wearing rubber knee high boots was obvious. By the time we dragged the boat up and dropped the anchor in the sand to keep the boat from drifting downriver, it was 10:45 p.m. But still daylight. Allen and I were still thinking on a college schedule as he was still wearing his wrist-watch.

The shore of the island, as well as the paths of camp which wound around through scrub willows, was sandy. Not the loose dry sand that you find at the beach or swimming recreation sites, but a hard-packed wet sand. Allen stated, "Camp could be a mess. They say very little snow last winter. The dry sand has blown away leaving this wet sand we walk on."

You couldn't really see the structures of camp itself from the boat on the shore because of the scrub willows. All you could see were the three radio antennas and the top of the net rack, a structure that Allen built to store their nets through the winter months so that they would not have to haul them back and forth between the camp and Mountain Village every spring and fall. The platform was about ten feet off the ground so that no spring flooding would wash the net away.

As we walked up the sandy path toward camp through the scrub willows, we passed a large sandy mound. Allen remarked, "A snow pile from last winter. Look at how the sand blew over it. We'll dig a hole in it and use it to store fish we want to eat," Allen said. I kicked at the mound with my rubber-booted toe and loosened the sandy covering to reveal pearl-white snow underneath.

The main part of the camp included two aluminum sheds, two small plywood-sided cabins, a steambath house, and a staked-out area where the kitchen tent would eventually be erected.

"We lock the houses when we are not here. People like to snoop around the camps of other people when the owners are not there. Sometimes they steal. All of our kitchen supplies, including the kitchen tent, are stored and padlocked in the little gray house."

The floor of the green house stood nearly six feet off the ground on huge stilt-like round poles. The smaller, grey house was only three or four feet off the ground.

"Why are they built up so high?"

"The houses? So that the spring floods, after the Yukon thaws, won't reach what's in them. You won't find another camp with these little wooden houses. We used to have tents like everyone else does at their fish camps. But we're at fish camp for nearly two months every summer. These little houses are a lot more protection from wind and rain than tents. I got the idea when they were building those newer houses in Mountain Village. I asked for scraps and I got them, the two-by-fours, plywood, and the aluminum."

"Pop didn't think it could be done. Moving these foundation logs was very hard work. At first, just Pop and I worked. Clyde and Leonard didn't believe it could be done either, but eventually they helped too. A lot of people are jealous of this place."

Allen's pride was clearly evidenced by his long discourse.

When I asked if they used electric tools, he replied, "Yes," and anticipated my next question by adding, "I have a Honda generator."

"How big are the houses?"

"The green house is sixteen-by-sixteen; the gray one twelve-by-twelve. When we all move down, you, me, and Clyde will sleep in the gray house. Everyone else, Mom and Pop and them, sleep in the green house. Leonard has his own tent. Donny usually sleeps with him."

He climbed the ten or so wooden steps of the green house and unlocked the padlock on the wooden door.

"The little gray house is full of stuff, so we'll sleep in this one tonight. Could be filthy—they say very little snow last year—much sand blew around."

His prediction proved to be accurate for a fine layer of dry silt and sand shrouded the floors, mattresses, cots, and everything stored on top of them.

We took everything out of the cabin, scattering the items around the camp, careful with those that would absorb moisture, like the mattresses and the sleeping bags. These we flopped onto the branches of scrub willows throughout the camp. Allen and I carried the heavy items, leaving only the wooden sleeping platforms. Mike, whom Allen usually called, "Quoo" moved the smaller items, knickknacks on the two-by-fours such as cans of bug spray, comic books, shotgun shells, and old rolls of toilet paper.

There is no sound like the Yup'ik "Q" in the English language and it is extremely difficult for English speakers who acquired English as a first language to pronounce. To the careless listener, the Yup'ik "Q" sounds like the English "K" or the English "Q", but it actually sounds more guttural than the English consonants. In English when the "K" sounds—"K", "Q", and the hard "C"—are produced, the back of the tongue comes in fairly close contact with the line between the hard palate and the velum, the soft palate. However, the sound of the Yup'ik "Q" is produced when the back of the tongue, even further back on the tongue than for the English "K", hits the soft palate or velum. The resulting sound is similar to a noise that one might make when trying to work up a spit. The Yup'ik "Q"as in Mike's Eskimo name, "Quoo," is extremely difficult for English speakers to produce.

When the cabin was almost empty, we attempted to sweep and dust the floors, walls, and ledges but soon found ourselves in a cloud of choking dust. There was no way to ventilate the room except for the lone door. The one small window, which allowed in scant light, was sealed so we could not open it to create circulation to move the filthy air out. When Mike and I exited out the door, coughing to clear our lungs, snorting to clear nasal passages, Allen, matter-of-factly, came up with a brilliant idea. Like most brilliant ideas, it was simple.

"Let's go across the river. There's moss on the other side. We'll use it to help absorb some of this dust and we can just sweep it out."

As we searched around the camp for buckets that we would use to transport the moss back across the river, I felt a nagging urge to relieve my bowels. Not wanting to violate some family or Yup'ik taboo, I asked, "Where's the outhouse?"

"We've been meaning to build one for several years but never got around to it. Too busy."

"Well what do you do when you gotta go?"

"Just go off in the trees a little ways—hang your dick out and piss!"

"Allen, I know that. I've gotta take a shit."

"Oh. Yeah. I'll find you some paper. I thought we took some out around here somewhere."

While he searched, I asked again, wanting to know what the protocol was for defecation at camp and not wanting to be offensive or violate any Yup'ik norms, "Where do you guys crap around here?"

When he returned and handed me the dusty roll, he answered me, "Same thing as pissing. You just go out a ways in the trees and squat. Kind of bury it by pushing dirt over it with your boot."

Wondering how this would work with a camp full of people, I asked, "Is this how you did it all summer? Even the women?"

Sometimes we sit in a honey bucket in one of the little houses."

"Whatsa honey bucket?"

Irritated with my ceaseless and what probably seemed to him to be stupid line of questioning by this time, he replied hotly, "A bucket we crap in!"

Still not getting the answer I wanted, I probed further, "What do they look like?"

Getting further aggravated by now, he replied, "You know—a plastic, white five gallon bucket. Like the one you're holding."

I looked at what I was holding. Earlier, before our toilet conversation, I found the bucket and thought it would be handy for holding moss. I had thought its dirty appearance was from dried mud. I looked at the bucket again and set it down. "I'm going to the trees."

Allen replied with a laugh this time, "It's kind of early now—but watch out for mosquitoes. Your hands will be busy."

I wasn't entirely sure what he meant that night, but weeks later when clouds of mosquitoes had hatched in the sloughs, dotting the tundra and spreading out to seek blood bearing victims as though they were some unearthly being found on a Star Trek episode, I did understand. During those weeks, with the tiny vampire population peaking in early to mid July, we lived in horror of the mosquito.

Those familiar with only the mosquito of the "lower forty-eight" cannot comprehend the Arctic mosquito. The seemingly docile creature I encountered while living in Oregon was tame when compared to the giant, tenacious critter that sought, and often successfully sucked my blood when I was in Alaska.

They came at you in swarms. This is especially hard to perceive when one considers that only female mosquitoes suck blood and do so in order to feed their eggs. During the early part of the summer, I wished for a tan, and roamed the camp in a t-shirt when the weather permitted and was loath to apply insect repellent. Soon I was covered with bites. The bites itched worse than those from mosquitoes I had previously encountered after my bites turned to scabs.

Not only is the Arctic mosquito much more tenacious than its southern cousins, she is larger and has a longer proboscis so that she can drill through corduroy or denim into skin, especially if the fabric is tight over the skin.

Fortunately, I wised up quickly before the tremendous swarms came. Those early spring mosquitos taught me valuable lessons. Even in the very rare eighty-degree weather, one always wore long sleeves. Something over the neck and head was also important. A jacket, such as a loose fitting kuspac, was necessary.

The kuspac was a very loose fitting pullover jacket with a large hood that can be pulled up tightly around the face. The men's warm weather kuspacs were made out of corduroy, light canvas, or denim and had a very large pocket stitched in the front across the chest. The large pocket was handy for storing cigarettes, chewing tobacco, matches, gloves, sandwiches, etc. The pocket had a zipper, perhaps eight-to-ten inches long, sewn diagonally across the chest for easy access.

The women's warmer weather kuspacs were usually sewn out of a lightweight cotton-printed fabric such as calico. These garments often had a ruffle around the bottom, and were much longer than the man's and hung nearly to the knees of the female wearer.

These kuspacs, homemade on sewing machines, were perfect garments to wear when working in summer weather around millions of mosquitoes. The combination of tightly woven fabric styled into loose fitting garments would not permit mosquito penetration, and the hood protected the neck, ears, all of the head, and some of the face. Winter kuspacs, made out of animal furs and skins, were similar in style to the summer ones. I recall many times seeing Allen's back covered in a shroud of angry mosquitos trying to probe through the corduroy fabric of his summer kuspac.

By wearing a kuspac, and, of course, long pants, you were almost completely protected from mosquitoes, except for your exposed face and hands. On these you applied "OFF" insect repellent, but most of the time your hands were covered with work gloves or fishing gloves. Dressed in this way, protection from mosquitoes was a maximum and bites were held to a minimum. Simple routine tasks were difficult, such as relieving bowels in the woods when your hands were too busy holding on to your pants to shoo away the clouds of mosquitoes, or even the act of changing your socks offered areas of juicy, tasty skin. Even "OFF" insect repellent was not very effective when working around camp, moving nets or wood, or chopping wood, for it seemed to rub off and you needed to re-dope yourself every thirty to forty-five minutes.

When we clambered into the boat to head across the river to gather moss for absorbing dust as we cleaned out the green house, Allen said, "Quoo. Go with Dan to find a short net close to shore here. Hopefully we'll catch something for dinner."

While we set the net, Mike said, "I wonder if them Philip are down." I asked Allen what Mike meant. He replied, "Phillip is building a little cabin on this island further back upriver. He wants to make a camp like ours. Let's go see if he's here."

With that he turned to Mike and said, as if to read his nephew's mind, "Quoo—maybe Jimmy there."

"Jimmy?" I asked.

"Jimmy is Quoo's older brother. He hangs around with Nook—Phillip, like Quoo here (put his arm around the boy) does with me."

Mike's "them Philip" usage intrigued me. As I listened carefully to this usage throughout the summer, I observed that "them" is used whenever someone refers to a specific group of people. In this creolized English, the speaker would label the group by naming the dominant person in the group, or perhaps the speaker's favorite person. Articles and words used to indicate a question were nearly always left out in a speech:

"Them Albert come back from store?"

"Eee-eee (yes). They go visit them Richard."

After setting the net, we cruised close to the shore of the island. Allen slowed the throttle when we sighted a beached boat. Phillip and Jimmy had finished building a platform about three feet high off the ground in a clearing they had made amid the scrub willows. The two pairs of brothers, Allen and Phillip, and Mike and Jimmy were glad to see each other. And I was introduced. Phillip and Jimmy had brought store-bought bread and peanut butter. Allen, Mike, and I were hungry.

Although a bit larger than Allen, Phillip closely resembled his younger brother in facial features and body build. He attended college in California to receive a degree in business administration and returned to Mountain Village to become the personnel director for the Lower Yukon School District, which holds its office there. He is a very articulate Eskimo, even more so than Allen, and has a unique combination of brother Clyde's gentle nature and the energetic on-the-go nature of Allen. He was very happy to hear of Allen's abstinence from alcohol.

After we parted, Allen, Mike, and I headed across the river toward the mosses on the opposite bank. At this point, the Yukon River is roughly a mile and a half across about some thirty miles from where it drains into the Bering Sea. When we reached the bank, Mike and I scrambled out of the boat and up the mossy bank, tore clumps of moss off, and threw the pieces down to the boat where Allen gathered them into the buckets.

The moss was perfect for cleaning out the house. We simply scattered it around the floors and ledges where the silt and sand was thickest. The moisture in the moss absorbed most of the dust and sand particles, and we swept moss as well as dust out of the house.

Finally, Allen located a Coleman stove and some propane. He needed coffee before bedtime. Because our set-net failed to catch a fish, we ate a Spartan meal of dry fish and Sailor-Boy-Pilot-Bread crackers. While we ate, Allen talked about some of the local medicinal remedies. He spoke of a local plant that grew on the tundra, caigglluk (pronounced "jygluck") that was used as a type of cure all. The leaves are boiled and the resulting juices are administered to people with bad colds. The leaves from caigglluk, also known as "skunk weed," are rubbed on skin ailments such as rashes and cuts. Allen rooted around in the cabin until he found an old peanut butter jar. He unscrewed the lid and pushed the jar towards my face. It contained a dark, thick liquid not unlike the tobacco juice one spits when having a chew of tobacco leaves. "Ciagglluk. Have a taste."

I took a small swig and found that it tasted bitter, not unlike tobacco juice.

Allen went on to describe another folk remedy. He explained to Mike and me that in older days they would cure T.B. (tuberculosis) by drinking the urine of a young boy. "Have young boy, like Mike, pee in a cup. Leave it to settle for a few hours then drink the top portion off. Supposed to cure T.B," he added.

As the three of us unrolled our sleeping bags, I reflected on the urine remedy for T.B. and wondered what other old cures I would learn. I looked at Allen's watch; the time was 4:00 a.m.

Chapter Seventeen
FRIENDS

We rose the next morning around 11:00, pulled in one small dog salmon off the set net, carried the cast-iron wood stove that Allen had purchased at G.I. Joe's in Oregon into one of the aluminum sheds, locked the two houses and shoved off from the camp toward Mountain Village.

When we arrived at Leonard's house, on the bank of the Yukon near Mountain Village, we learned that Clyde had gotten drunk the previous night and wrecked the clutch and transmission in his dad's pickup. Since Leonard wrecked his Bronco while almost everyone else was "outside" at Clara's graduation, the family was without a running vehicle. The mile and a half walk from the river to Papa Joseph Green's house seemed very long when carrying armloads of jackets and bags. Allen told me sarcastically, "It's the cool thing here – to go out and get drunk and wreck vehicles. Just watch, they'll let Dad pay for the truck and go out and wreck it again."

So far, I felt more of a burden to Allen than a help. Later that evening, however, after eating a hearty supper of moose stew and homemade biscuits, Allen asked me to wrap his wrist which he injured pounding a fishing hole through the ice on the river during the spring break.

"I'm glad you're here, Dan. You're the only one who understands me."

As I looked at him speaking to me, I realized that he was truly a man walking between two worlds. Some of the younger people from the village did, indeed, treat him like he thought he was too good for them but Allen went right along saying "hi" to everyone. If they were people he liked, he would introduce me; if not, we departed quickly.

Allen added, "You're not afraid of hard work. Things will slow down once we're settled at camp."

Chapter Eighteen
CULTURAL CONTINUITY

Both Allen and Clara's career passions were to gain college teaching degrees and return to their home village to educate the youth in the Yup'ik culture and language. They were very concerned about the increasing loss of their culture and language in their people, particularly the youth.

There are three generations of Yup'iks in the 1970s through 1990s to review when discussing culture change. The oldest generation, I refer to as the First Generation. These were the elders in the Yup'ik families and communities: the grandparents and great-grandparents, like Joseph and Arlene Green. Many of these elders, such as Papa Joseph, were fluent in only one language, Yup'ik. They spoke only a smattering of English words. They were experienced in the ancient traditions of the Yup'ik culture that were passed down orally from generation to generation.

The Second Generation are Alaska's adult working force today. They are the children of the First Generation, such as Allen, Clara, Clyde, and their siblings. This group of people grew up learning Yup'ik as their first language and acquired English as their second language while they attended Catholic missionary and BIA (Bureau of Indian Affairs) schools scattered throughout the region. Allen, Clara, and Clyde attended the Catholic mission school in St. Mary's and roomed in the school's dormitories while attending school.

When the Second Generation, Allen, his peers, and siblings, started in the BIA schools, they brought with them their language, the only language they could speak, and their Yup'ik culture, only to find that they were punished physically and emotionally by their teachers forcing them to abandon their Yup'ik ways and adopt the Anglo-American culture and language. Some teachers went as far as to put tape over the mouths of children who spoke Yup'ik in the classroom.

As the Second Generation grew to be the adult working force and began to have children of their own, they remembered how useless their Yup'ik language and culture were in the school environment. Accordingly, they taught their children English only and not the Yup'ik language and culture. This Third Generation, children like Donnie Green and his cousins and peers, were fluent in English by the time they reached school age and knew only a few Yup'ik words. The emphasis on English and the Anglo-American culture in schools further marginalized the significance of their ancestral culture.

The result, after assimilation of Yup'ik children into the mainstream language and culture was a huge cultural gap between the generations with the threat of Yup'ik language and culture extinction. For example, Grandpa Joseph Green, fluent only in Yup'ik, could not tell his grandsons, Donnie and Jimmy, who were fluent only in English, the spiritual significance involved in taking a fire bath or "mukie." An elder could not teach grandchildren how to hunt and fish and care for game in respectful ways. Traditional storytelling and other means of sharing culture could not occur because elders and youth did not share a common language.

The Second Generation of Alaskan Natives are a talented group of people. They are equally comfortable and fluent in both Yup'ik and English languages and cultures. They are the bridge between the old traditions and the emerging technologies. Alaskans are a people who exist in two worlds. They recognize that their cultural traditions can become extinct if their children, the Third Generation, would not be able to pass on the Yup'ik language, and subsequently transfer knowledge about the culture to the next generation. Anthropologists have long observed that the extinction of a culture's language signals its coming death.

Over the years, the Second Generation went through a lot of soul searching. They questioned the importance of retaining their culture. Some have even asked, "Why bother?" As a group, however, they decided that retaining their culture is important because it enhances young peoples' positive feelings about themselves, their culture, and their future existence as a people.

In response to this, in 1976 the Lower Kuskokwim School District, the largest school district in southwestern Alaska, the land of the Yup'ik Eskimo, developed the Yup'ik-as-a-Second-Language curriculum (YSL) (Collier 1). The basic premise for YSL was that Yup'ik was taught as a second language in the hopes that keeping the language alive to some degree may sustain the culture (Jacobson 19).

With the introduction of YSL programs into school districts comprised largely of Yup'ik Eskimos, the Second Generation took positive steps to ensuring the preservation of their culture and language. Thus, a grandfather speaking Yup'ik as a first language and his grandson speaking Yup'ik as a second language will hopefully be able to communicate with each other and continue the language and the culture. The program resulted in only limited success through the years, partly because it is not reinforced outside of the school. One hopes that no group, ever again, is forced to acquire a new language and culture and push aside, subvert, and forget about their own first language and culture in the same manner that the Alaska Native adult working force did as students in these BIA schools during the 1940s to the early 1970s.

Chapter Nineteen
CROSSING THE WILD RIVER

Several days later, the majority of Allen's family, his parents, Clara, MaryAnn, their children, and Clyde—were ready to make the trek together downriver to fish camp. This trek was not a simple visit or check-over as Allen and I had done earlier to check over the condition of camp and supplies. Large quantities of food staples were purchased at the village store. The extra blankets, clothes, and sufficient cooking supplies had to last several weeks until we had a chance to visit the store again for more supplies. We were essentially moving from Mountain Village to fish camp for the summer.

While we loaded the boats, I noticed Papa Joseph, rummaging around in the weeds on the steep bank of the river. When he had found what he was looking for, he stood up and his hands held a battered snowmobile seat cushion. Curious as to what he wanted with that old piece of junk, I watched quietly at a distance as he struggled on very bowed, arthritic legs down the bank to his boat. There he laid the cushion on the floor of the boat. Then his wife, Arlene, climbed into the boat and settled herself on the ragged cushion.

Not one word has passed between Arlene and Joseph during this entire scene. Yet I sensed that some communication had occurred. Eskimos are traditionally short on conversation and long on action. While thinking of the little scene between this old couple, I remembered Allen telling me once, "In our culture, when you want someone to know how you feel about them, you don't tell them. You show them. When someone does something nice for you, you do something nice for them in return. You show them how you feel. You don't tell them. In our culture, showing is viewed as a much more genuine sign of feeling than telling."

I have often wondered if Joseph and Arlene ever told each other that they loved each other. I guess it didn't really matter because they were never separated and often showed each other. They both knew how the other felt about each other. Part of this wasn't necessarily a Yup'ik thing but a generational thing. Several of the older couples in my own family of that generation related to each other in a similar manner.

After we finished loading the boats, we pushed off from the bank and slowly throttled down to the watering area where the freshwater spring flowed off some rocks through a pipe and into the Yukon. We brought with us several large clean plastic garbage cans for the sole purpose of water storage. We filled these cans as well as a half a dozen ten gallon jugs and began our journey downriver toward camp.

Clara, Allen, and I rode in Allen's boat. Because Allen's boat was the largest of the three, we carried the water and the heaviest load. MaryAnn, and her two-year old daughter, Lucy, rode with the folks in the boat that MaryAnn and her father, Papa Joseph, shared for fishing. They also had two large mongrel dogs, Tiger and Tootsie with them in their boat along with the food supplies, personal clothing, and camping gear. The dogs apparently were at ease riding in these wooden flat-bottom boats on rough waters for they strained at their ropes tied to the seats trying to peer over the edge of the bow to get the full effect of the spray.

When we reached the point of the trip where the smaller stream behind a group of smaller, skinny islands flows into the main branch of the river, we saw that the river was wild with huge waves. The wind had picked up fiercely since we had left Mountain Village an hour ago. We had to cross the breadth of the wide Yukon with those mighty waves in order to reach the camp on the other side. I could not determine where the camp was nor could I see the three CB radio antennas that marked our camp. The family, however, knew exactly where to cross to make the trip the shortest distance.

Allen's father, Joseph, led our little caravan of boats across the water. From years of experience, the wily old river man could read his river with more scrutiny than most people read their emails. He could tell by looking at the surface of the water and the shape of the waves, where submerged sandbars were, and where the swift deep running currents were. These areas were ever changing so a river man had to be prepared to respond to these changes.

Joseph Green started his boat across twice with us following and stopped twice. Finally, he led us across slowly zig-zagging to absorb the minimum impact of the waves, but careful not to turn too much to prevent the waves from swamping the boat. At times, his craft looked to be tipped at a 45 degree angle with the two dogs continuing to strain at their ropes looking over the bow nearly ten feet higher than Joseph, Arlene, MaryAnn, and Lucy who were huddled at the stern near the kicker.

As we crossed, water splashed over the sides of the boat and splattered all the plastic sheeting protecting our gear. I realized why Allen told me to wear rain overall bibs on this trip even though no rain clouds could be seen. They knew it was going to be a rough trip, although had they known it to be this rough, I doubt they would have attempted it.

I glanced at Allen's water-splashed shotgun propped next to him near the kicker and understood why it was so rusted.

Much of the rest of the summer was spent on the water in Allen's boat, but I'll never forget that intense and exhilarating trip. Later during the commercial fishing season, the water became so rough at times that we didn't go near the boats other than to check that they were securely staked down yet the water never seemed rougher than the day we crossed the mighty lower Yukon for our summer move to fish camp.

Chapter Twenty

SETTING UP CAMP

One of the first things that Papa Green did when we finally reached the island camp was to stake the dogs out with each one positioned on opposite sides of the camp. We were so busy setting up camp that I didn't think about why the dogs were along on the trip, or why they were staked out. Several days later, Clara, who somehow knew of my nocturnal trips to relieve myself, warned me against the habit with wide eyes.

"Dan. You been going out of your house at night?" Allen, Clyde, and I slept in the little twelve-foot-by-twelve foot shack.

"Yes. I usually need to pee. Why?"

"Don't do that anymore. Sometimes we have bears wander around the camp at night. That's why Papa lets the dogs out at night—to help keep the bears away and maybe warn us of them."

"Clara—why are they staked up at all?"

"To keep them out of mischief. They are very mean dogs."

Throughout the summer, I realized that dogs were not pets for Yup'ik Eskimos. They had specific purposes for owning dogs. Some were used as sled dogs. Others, such as these, were used for bear deterrents.

Clara's tales of bears, told with a very serious expression and wide eyes, were enough to convince me to abandon my nightly excursions outside the shack. But I had to do something about the nocturnal bladder urge and procured an old plastic ice cream pail. Allen also used it as a spittoon for his first chew in the mornings.

Naturally curious, I had to find out how mean the dogs really were. I've always enjoyed animals. I approached Tiger as he was chained to a log. He growled and curled his lips. And when I reached a particular distance from him, he lunged at

Boys playing in the water near the docked boats on a rare warm summer day. Notice how wide the Yukon River is here. The Green family fish camp is on an island in the Yukon River.

me to the length of the chain, snapping his fangs. Then I approached the female, Tootsie, at the other end of camp, with similar caution, and got the same response that Tiger had given me. It was enough to convince me to leave them alone.

Later that summer, Papa staked out Tootsie on the soft, sandy shore of the Yukon River. I couldn't figure out why he made this move.

I made a habit to check on Tootsie everyday. Soon Clara gave me old moldy dryfish to feed the dog instead of doing it herself. I observed Tootsie's den dug out of the sandy bank getting a little larger everyday until it was large enough so that she could completely disappear into the hole. The only sign of her was her chain leading her into the hole. Finally Tootsie had her pups in the protection of her little cave.

I watched daily as the pups grew. Eventually Tootsie let me hold them. One day, however, when the pups would have been about two weeks old, they disappeared. I asked Donnie if he knew where they were. He flatly replied, "Papa (his grandfather, Joseph) drowned them."

I guess it made sense. There are no vets in rural Alaska to do spaying or neutering, so euthanasia was the only way to take care of unwanted pups.

Setting up camp our first day there was an all-out effort. The heavy water barrels had to be dragged up and placed in one of the aluminum sheds. The kitchen stove, a very small, primitive, cast-iron wood-burner, was muscled out of the smaller shack. It was used for storage during the winter months. The kitchen tent was also pulled out of the shack and set up along with a picnic table and benches for the inside of the tent. Until we had wood, we'd be unable to use any of the stoves either for cooking or for the heat. Until we had wood, Clara and Ma (Arlene) cooked on a Coleman stove. Driftwood for fuel was essential for life at camp.

Almost everyone worked efficiently to get camp in order. I pitched in where I could. After storage items were pulled from the little shack, I readied the shack for Allen, Clyde, and I to sleep in by throwing everything out and sweeping out all the winter accumulation of dust, silt, and sand as Allen and I had done previously

We are getting ready for a meal. The kitchen tent has not been set up yet. Arlene "Mama" Green is wearing a summer weight kuspak. The two small cabins where we slept can be seen in the upper left of the photo in the background through the early spring willow trees.

with the larger shack. Then I laid the two old, holey, double mattresses down on the floor boards with our sleeping bags on top. Allen's was in the middle between Clyde's on one side of the shack and mine on the other. Everyone else would sleep in the large shack. Next I moved our duffle bags of clothes into the little shack.

While most of us worked, huge Donnie teased little Lucy and Mike, who frolicked nearly naked on the beach. Clyde quietly surveyed the activities while sitting on a log chain-smoking Marlboros.

After I emerged from my house cleaning duties, Clara informed me that we needed a trash pit. For a while I worked on this by digging into the sandy soil with the camp spade. It felt good to have a certain familiarity of using a spade and digging amidst all the new experiences I was being exposed to.

As I finished the construction of the trash pit, Allen hollered at me to get my rubber knee high boots on; we were to get fire wood. Since there are no sizeable trees in the lower Yukon River region, firewood is found by cruising the shores of the river to search for suitable wood that had drifted down from way upriver. I was amazed at the ability of the family to spot good firewood even from a distance. I would point, "how about that one" and get a response, "too wet" or "too green" or "ok for cooking or steam bath, but not good enough for drying fish."

The family practically lived in their rubber knee high boots during the summer months because many times one was forced to wade in shallow water to pull or push a boat. Boating on the Yukon can be a very wet affair, with the frequent rains and rough waters, so the boots are crucial for dry feet. My feet sweat so much, even with absorbent wool socks, that my feet were wet anyway. We also wore our boots while walking in the tundra, which is often quite marshy.

Allen grabbed the chainsaw, and soon we were on the river searching for wood. After cruising on the water for a while, he spied some promising wood for cooking and for a steam bath. He cut the throttle as the boat drifted to nudge the bank. As quick as a cat, he snatched the chainsaw, and in three fast steps he was out of the boat. I was considerably slower, as I had still not found my water legs. By the time I was out of the boat and reached Allen, he had two chunks of log sawed and ready to be transported back to the boat.

After a couple of hours of scouring the shores for wood and stopping to cut logs into moveable chunks, we arrived back at camp with a sizable load of wood. Clyde and Papa Joseph helped Allen and I carry the wood up to the sawhorse near the middle of camp. During the afternoon of repeated scrambling from the boat to shore and back from shore with loads of wood, I slowly adapted to gaining the

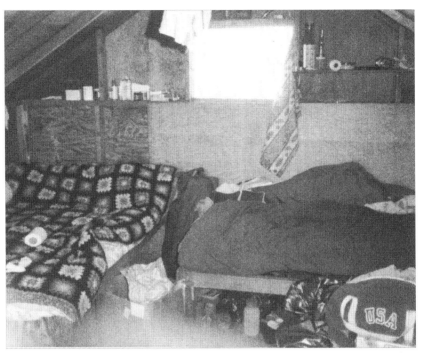

Inside the 16 foot by 16 foot plywood sleeping cabin, where most of the family slept while at Fish Camp.

coordination of a river man.

Allen chain-sawed the cut log-chunks into even smaller pieces and told me to start splitting them. As soon as we had four split pieces, Allen grabbed them and headed towards the steam bath house.

"I'm going to start a steam. You'll see how we clean ourselves at camp, Dan. Keep splitting the wood and stack it over there. Clyde, keep sawing those logs up for Dan to split."

He was clearly the camp boss and answered to no one, not even his older siblings, only to his father, Joseph.

Chapter Twenty-One
STEAM BATH

Several hours later, Allen announced that the steam bath was ready. The steam bath house was a low dwelling, built like a tiny cabin, but perhaps five feet wide by ten feet long and five feet high at the peak. The whole structure was constructed out of plywood and two-by-fours.

I crawled through the doorway on my hands and knees found myself in a tiny room, perhaps only two feet long and the width of the shack. There was a narrow bench on the sides of both walls.

"This is the cooling room, Dan. Take your clothes off."

My bare left shoulder brushed the wooden wall on my left as I sat down on the narrow bench, naked and across from the equally naked Allen. The wall was hot to touch. A little wooden sliding door, about the same size as the door one enters the structure from the outside indicated the entrance into the steam room, the main room of the tiny structure.

Allen carried a large bowl with him and a bar of soap. We swung our clothes outside the little building and on top of its low roof, efficiently out of the way in our cramped situation.

"We splash three times, usually. In between splashes, we come out here and cool down. When we go for our last splash, we soap our whole body down and let the sweat and steam run the soap off our bodies. You'll be cleaner than after you've had a shower, Dan. All your pores will be clean because the sweating causes the dirt to come out of them. Your pores don't get clean when you just take a shower." While wondering just exactly what Allen meant by a splash, he got on his hands and knees and slid the door open to the steam room. As he did this, heat blasted out like it does when you open the door of a hot oven. Allen scrambled through and snapped, "Hurry up, Dan. We want to keep as much heat in here as possible."

The interior of the steam room was perhaps eight feet long, and hotter than any sauna I had ever been in previously. The wooden floor ended about two feet from the back of the room to allow for a pit in which lay a fifty-five gallon metal barrel on its side. Allen fed the fire in it through a hole in one of the ends. A stove pipe led up from the top of the metal barrel through the roof, exhausting the smoke from the fire to the outside of the steam bath house.

Rocks were built up all around the outside of the barrel. We seated ourselves on small benches along the walls. Allen picked up a stick from the floor; on one end of the stick a tin can was tied in place with twine. Allen dipped this into a metal bucket, filling the can with water, and splashed the water onto the hot rocks positioned on top of the makeshift stove. Immediately hot steam billowed over us.

We sat there in silence for a while. The moist heat felt good on my tired, aching body, and finally forced me to relax. Soon I almost felt drugged; I was so relaxed that I couldn't contemplate being anywhere else at that moment.

"You'll really appreciate this after a cold, wet, twenty-four hour fishing period." With that, he made another splash, which made the room even hotter.

As we sat absorbing the moist heat, Allen said, "We get this water from the Clearwater sloughs back off the Yukon. Yukon water has too much silt in it, and it dries on the rocks, the silt gets all over the place in here and makes a mess. And our drinking water, the water we get by the spring up by Mountain Village, is much too valuable here at camp to use for steam bath splashes."

He splashed again. This time the steam became so hot, I could barely breathe; the inside of my nostrils burned from the heat. I dipped my towel in the water and held the wet towel over my face so that I could breathe easier. My skin felt like it was burning and drowning at the same time. My dirty pores exploded their blockage. My body was completely soaked from my own sweat and I felt as if I were boiling in it. Finally I couldn't take the heat anymore.

"I gotta get out, Allen."

He laughed and replied, "We'll toughen you up, Dan. In a few weeks, you'll be able to take a lot more steam heat than you can now. Maybe as much as me."

After I escaped into the tiny cooling room, Allen splashed again. I could hear him screaming, "I—I—I—I" through the walls and door that separated us. Finally, he opened the door and crawled through yelling, "echi-echi" (good-good). He babbled other Yup'ik words and seemed like he was about to pass out. I reached over to touch his skin. It was piping hot! He lay there, collapsed on the floor, with his heart beating furiously. I could see his pulse in his neck. He barely had enough strength to spit.

As he lay there, I became a little concerned. After all I had been bicycling rigorously for several years. My cardiovascular system was superior to his—or was it? Allen had spoken of men in their late seventies "taking really hot ones," with no heart attacks. Eskimos rarely die of heart attacks. I thought that perhaps one needed to become acclimated in order to tolerate a good, long and hot steam bath.

Allen crawled off the floor and over to his little bench opposite me and pushed open the outside door. A cool breeze drifted in and over our hot, moist skin. Only mosquito netting, separated us from the cool, outside air. Struggling against the netting to gain their freedom to the outside, were two fat mosquitoes bulging red with our blood. I snatched one and squashed it. Its blood or rather Allen's or my blood, spattered all over my fingers.

"Our skin is desensitized from the steam bath. We can't feel them bite."

With that, he reached outside to grasp his kuspak, pulled it in, and unzipped the oversized pocket. I thought he was reaching for his Copenhagen, but to my surprise he pulled out a pack of Marlboros and a lighter. As if to respond to my questioning face, he stated, "If I smoke, the bugs leave us alone."

He was right. And it was the only time in my life that I was thankful to be in the presence of cigarette smoke.

Within twenty minutes, our naked bodies were completely dry and cool. So we entered the steam room again and repeated the whole splashing, steaming, and cooling process two more times. I learned that a "splash" meant a single duration of time spent in the steam room, regardless of how many times water is splashed on the rocks. On our third splash, we soaped our bodies. When the steam really began rolling, Allen asked if I could feel my pores popping the dirt out.

I could.

Chapter Twenty-two
NETS AND SUBSISTENCE FISHING

T he next morning I awoke to the smell of pancakes and found myself rested and alone in the tiny cabin for Allen and Clyde had already risen. After I dragged on my clothes and stumbled out of the cabin over to the kitchen tent, I entered through the flaps to find Ma flipping a pancake on the cast-iron grill top on the little wood-burning stove. Its pipe rose through a hole in the roof of the tent.

She must have mixed enough batter to feed a football team because I found myself gluttonously downing seven medium sized pancakes. Everyone else was also well-fed. Allen said, "You're not finished eating until you're filled and all the food is gone." No wonder he could fit two-hundred pounds into his five-foot four-inch frame. I would gain ten pounds on my skinny frame that summer.

Allen, his brothers, and his father all bought their nets from the village store. They didn't like the way the nets were "hung," the method in which the float and weighted lines were stitched to the main part of the net in the factory where they were made. So, the Greens removed the float and the weight lines from the net and "re-hung" them, claiming that the way they "hung" the nets enabled them to gain larger catches than the way the factory "hung" them.

Allen led me to a wooden platform approximately ten feet off the ground and supported with four long posts. "We put our nets up here so that we don't have to transport them up from Mountain Village in the spring and back down in the fall. We built this platform up high so that the water from the river melting in the spring won't carry the nets away."

Author Dan Syljuberget on top of the net scaffol in fish camp.*

We climbed up a ladder to the top of the platform made of branches and scrap wood, and found his king salmon net amid a massive confusion of nets. As we moved the net down to the ground, Allen explained, "When handling nets, Dan, you must keep the weighted side separated from the float side. Otherwise you can have a mess."

He further explained that they used two different types of nets throughout the course of the summer. The net we were carrying, stretched over our shoulders, had an eight and three-quarter inch mesh and was designed specifically to catch the largest salmon species—king salmon. The large mesh holes allowed the smaller fish a means of escape. The "king" net was legally allowed to be used commercially only during king salmon season which was a period three to four weeks as designated by the Alaska Fish and Game Department. We would fish commercially to sell to fish collectors who cruised the river looking for small boats, such as ours. The fish collectors, in turn, resold the fish to canneries or drove down the Yukon to the Bering Sea to sell to Japanese fishing ships. Frequently, a fish collector boat might be affiliated with a particular cannery or fishery firm.

But on that day, we were not going to be fishing commercially; we would be fishing for subsistence to stock up for the family's winter supply of fish. I would experience my first taste of both fishing with a net and fresh Alaska Yukon River salmon.

We laid the net in the boat with the float side on one side of the front bench seat and the weight side on the other side of this same seat, then tied the end to boat. Between the two wooden bench seats, Allen had placed a huge plastic tub, which he called a "tote." The tote would hold our catch.

We clambered into the boat and Allen throttled us away.

When we reached a certain place in the river, straight in front of camp and on the other side of a large sandbar, Allen cut the throttle of the fifty-horse Evinrude and started up the smaller kicker, a fifteen-horse Mariner. He hollered at me to throw out the end-float, a huge bright pink plastic ball-shaped float about two and a half feet in diameter. This float marked the end of the net line and could be spotted from a long distance.

I threw it out over the water as far as I could and soon found that you should not stand on any other parts of the net remaining in the boat when you are letting the net out of the boat. As the float pulled the net out into the water, my inexperienced feet were nearly knocked out from under me because I had naively been standing on it.

Allen steadied the throttle handle of the small kicker, steered the boat to the position he wanted, and jumped over to the fast moving net, "You gotta really watch the net, Dan, otherwise the float side will tangle up with the weight side when you let it out."

With each hand, he grasped both sides of the net, the float side and the weight side, and guided the net on its journey over the edge of the boat and into the water. When he was satisfied with the way the net was traveling out of the boat, he marched back to the kicker and operated it from a standing position with one foot relaxed on the bench seat, the other leg supporting his weight. He stood like this with his body position quite relaxed, as he had grown up in boats, and barked orders to me about controlling the net as it traveled out of the boat.

The river was fairly calm that day, and the weather was quite mild and sunny. We wore caps, light jackets, sweaters, jeans, and the ever-present rubber knee-high boots. My legs were beginning to adapt to standing and moving around in a drifting boat on active waters. I felt much more at ease today, especially after gaining experience moving in and out of the boat for gathering wood the previous day, than I did on my first boat ride to collect rhubarbs. And yet, with my fledgling attempts to handle the net, I knew I had a lot more to learn.

When the net had stretched over the water to reach its total length, we sat

The drift net ready to be let out into the river for a drift. The weighted line for the bottom of the net is in the lower left corner of the photo, while the floate♦ top of the net is in the mi♦♦le of the photo an♦ the main float in the top right of the photo. Allen an♦ his father crafted this boat from lumber.

calmly on our respective benches. I was near the bow of the boat where the net was tied; Allen sat near the kicker. We were quiet. We just sat there feeling the sun on our faces and the current gently rocking the boat. Allen motioned to me to look at the net because the fish, caught near the top of the net, broke the surface of the water as they flopped around struggling to gain their freedom.

After drifting for roughly a mile to where Allen had a spot marked on the shore, he declared it was time to pull the net in. He grabbed his rubber Helly-Hansen rain pants, which come clear up to the chest and are held up by elastic suspenders. I too pulled mine on as we located our fishing gloves which were cheap yellow cotton gloves with a webbing of plastic glued over the palms and fingers. Allen said these were the cheapest and best to use for handling fish. Although they would protect our hands from cuts and punctures that came from handling fish, they offered little protection from the icy water. I never did get used to slipping my hands into those frigid, wet gloves on a cold wet day.

We both stood on opposite sides of the front bench seat near the bow, the one that I sat on when we drifted or traveled. Allen grabbed the weighted line and began pulling the net into the boat and ordered me to do the same with the float side. Again the two sides of the net were separated over the bench. A net filled with salmon, and pulled into a boat by hand is heavy—very heavy.

It was quickly apparent why Allen always would choose the weight side of the net to pull in and delegated the float side for me to handle. Most of the fish were caught toward the bottom of the net. It takes a balance of skill and experience to untangle a fish from the net. The harder they fight the more tangled on the net they become. Allen had been untangling salmon from nets for over twenty years; he was an expert. I, on the other hand, was again the greenhorn. At first, the confusion of tangles and snarls seemed hopelessly frustrating, but as I worked through the summer, side-by-side with Allen, watching him carefully, I matured and became more confident. In time, I would stand, next to Allen in torrential rains and winds, on river-worthy legs, and with a strong back and nimble fingers.

Chapter Twenty-three
DRY FISH

In that single drift we landed one-hundred thirty-eight chum salmon and six king salmon. We had plenty in our tote. As we steered back towards the shore by our camp, I noticed that during our absence, a homemade table had been set up on the beach near the water's edge. Papa and Ma Green, along with Clara, stood

Salmon strips hanging in the fish house

Arlene "Mama" and Joseph "Papa" Green prepare salmon for drying. Note upper right of photo where salmon will hang for two days before being transported to a more closed shed to dry for two weeks.

waiting, armed with ulu knives. The traditional ulu knife has a blade shaped like a half-moon and is secured to a handle carved out of bone or wood by leather thongs, screws or nails.

I watched in awe as Ma and Clara skillfully prepared the salmon for drying. Clara first chopped off the head of her salmon, and with a poke of the sharp corner of her ulu knife into the anal vent, she sliced up the belly of the fish. After she and Ma finished de-heading and gutting the entire catch, they moved the salmon up the bank closer to the camp and a very large cutting table. While they did this, Allen and I gathered the guts and heads into buckets and drove out to the middle of the river and dumped them.

A fire, which served as a mosquito deterrent, burned quite close to the cutting table where Clara and Ma now worked. The women cut and filleted the salmon lengthwise parallel to the spine so that only the tail held the two sides of the fish together. Then they made horizontal cuts across the meat on the inside of the two sides to enable the fish to dry better and to make the meat easier to tear off from the skin for eating.

When we hung the fish on the horizontal poles supported about five feet off the ground by other poles in an open-air shed, it quickly became apparent why the tails were left on. The salmon were simply draped over the poles with the tail sticking up perpendicular from the pole with the two sides of the fish dangling down from each side of the pole.

Three days later, Ma deemed the fish sufficiently aired and we transported them to a closed shed made out of corrugated aluminum which had holes punched in the walls for air circulation. Again, the fish were hung on horizontal poles. Allen built a fire in an old metal drum partially buried in the sandy floor of the shed. "The fire," he said, "must burn continuously for the duration of the drying process" (actually smoking the salmon). "Only cottonwood is burned as it gives

Salmon drying in an aluminum-sided fish house where they will hang for two weeks over a smoking pit of burning cottonwood. Joseph Green peers over the top of the dry-fish salmon. Notice the upper part of the photo where salmon strips hang, which are cut differently from the dry-fish.

the fish its best flavor," claimed Ma. Until the drying process was complete, one of the most important camp activities, aside from constantly checking and feeding the fire, was cruising the river to gather cottonwood drifting down from miles upriver. Chain sawing and splitting the wood also occupied our time for wood was needed, not only for the smoke house, but also for the camp stoves and the steam bath.

The fish hung in the smoke house for two weeks until Ma declared that the fish were sufficiently dried and flavored. Then the fish were taken down and stacked very tightly into wooden barrels lined on the inside with plastic bags. The barrels had to be as air-tight as possible to lessen the amount of mold that would develop in the winter months. The barrels would be opened, as needed to obtain the fish, starting in October; the dry fish would be eaten as subsistence through the winter into next summer. The dry fish we ate now was smoked and stored the previous summer.

Chapter Twenty-four
FIRE BATH

One afternoon, after we had just finished several hours of gathering, chopping, and splitting wood, we checked in the smoke house and Allen declared, "It's time for you to take a fire bath."

"What's a fire bath?"

"That is what they used to take in the older days before the people started building and using steam baths."

"Are we going to build one?"

"No, Papa has one further back on the island. He very, very seldom takes a steam bath; he prefers the old way, the fire bath. Come."

He led me into the kitchen tent where Papa was sitting on the floor carving long shavings from a willow stick. When Papa was satisfied with the pile of shaving strips between his knees, he laid down the knife and the naked stick, and gathered the wood shaving strips into bundles, each one roughly five inches long. Around this bundle, he wrapped a square of old canvas and secured it with twine.

"What's that?"

"For muckie."

Allen explained, "He means for fire bath. Muckie means fire bath in Yup'ik. The bundle of willow branch shavings is a muckie stick. We use them to breath through so that the smoke from the fire won't hurt our lungs."

As I asked more questions, I learned that the fire bath is an ancient Yup'ik ritual of body and mind cleanliness. The popularity of the steam bath, however, had almost made the fire bath a practice of the past.

The fire bath turned out to be a small and very short hut built from logs and was roughly ten feet long and five feet wide, about three feet higher near the

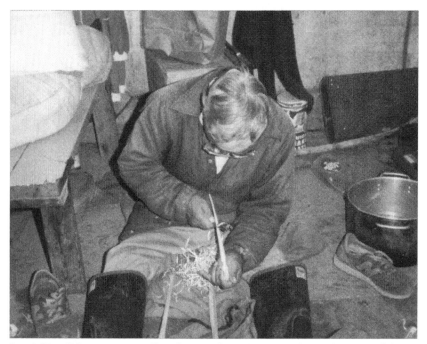

Joseph "Papa" Green cutting willow shavings for making a muckie stick. Users of the fire bath or "muckie" breathe through these to filter out the smoke from the fire.

entrance sloping to four feet high near the back. After stripping and leaving our clothes outside, we entered through a very small door. Once inside the very tiny structure, I could see a pit near the back wall about two and a half feet deep into the soil, similar to the fire pit in ground of the smoke house.

Allen built a fire in the pit and some of its smoke rose out of square holes cut in the roof of the low hut. When the fire was really roaring, Allen produced two old wool stocking caps.

"What are these for?"

"You have to wear these caps in here so that your hair, ears, eyelids, and eyebrows won't singe."

While I contemplated burning hair, Allen handed me one of the "muckie sticks" and demonstrated by sticking his in his mouth and sucking through it like a huge cigarette. I found that by breathing through the willow shavings of the muckie stick, the smoke was indeed filtered out. I also put a wet rag over the end of my stick to cool the hot air. With all this apparatus to breathe through, my lungs labored for breath. My eyes smarted from the smoke so I pulled the cap down over them. Thankfully, the smoke kept the mosquitoes away.

In spite of the discomfort I felt while my body sweated, like my experience earlier in the steam bath, I found that the fire bath caused the tensions of the day to melt away. Allen told me, perhaps mostly to make me feel good, that not many "outsiders" could tolerate the effects of the fire bath for as long as we did that day.

Chapter Twenty-five
GOING TO THE SANDBAR

After cooling off from the fire bath and indulging in a snack of dry fish and Sailor-Boy-Pilot-Bread crackers, Clara suggested to Allen that we boat out to the large sandbar in the river in front of the camp to fly Allen's large kite that he purchased at an Oregon coast kite store. The huge sandbar was permanent enough that it had a number of small scrub willow trees growing on it. After we lofted Allen's kite and tied it down, Allen and I played catch with the baseball and a pair of gloves, which traveled with me everywhere. The kids, Lucy, Zachary, Mike, and Jimmy, chased each other, while Clara and her younger sister, MaryAnn, talked quietly about school in Oregon.

After a while, Clara, Allen, and I walked along the length of the sandbar island. MaryAnn went to check on little Lucy. The three of us reminisced about events and people we had encountered over the past two years of living in Monmouth, Oregon. It was a time to relax, to share, to remember, and to wind-down from all the hustle and bustle of the past several weeks. Soon the commercial fishing season would open and we all would be busy again. The discussion turned towards the future with Clara saying that Allen had better find a wife during the next school year. Allen agreed. Clara further added that she was going back to school when Donnie reached high school age so that he could go to school in Oregon. As we walked along talking, Clara blurted out suddenly, "Auntie—Auntie." I looked around and saw only Jimmy.

"What was that all about Clara?"

"I always wanted Jimmy to call me 'Auntie', but he won't, so I call him 'Auntie'."

We all laughed as we walked back to the boat.

Chapter Twenty-Six
COMMERCIAL FISHING

The weather was unusually warm, calm, and clear for the commercial fishing season opener. The first run of fish included the major run of the king salmon, called "Chinook" in some regions. Kings, which ranged from seven to sixty pounds and averaging about twenty five pounds at $1.50 a pound, were the moneymaker for Lower Yukon River fishermen. "If you don't have a good king season, you will end up with a poor summer," Allen informed me.

During king season, the dates of which are controlled by Alaska Fish and Wildlife Service, all commercial fishermen were required to use only nets with an eight and three-quarter inch mesh to allow escapement for the smaller kings. Chum salmon were also allowed to be harvested during king season. "Dogs," as the Yup'iks called the chum salmon, yielded thirty cents a pound and averaged around six pounds in weight.

Because there were four groups, four boats—Allen's, Clyde's, Leonard's, and MaryAnn's and her father's, we had to set up a rotation of turns to drift the traditional spot between the huge sandbar and the deep main channel of the Yukon. When one group pulled in their net, another would start their drift.

We worked all day gathering, sawing, splitting, and stacking firewood for the smoke house and kitchen stove. I was tired by the 6:00 p.m. time of the official opening. In anticipation of this opening day, I didn't sleep the previous night. We would be fishing until 6:00 p.m. the next day—twenty-four hours of fishing—and about forty hours without rest before going to bed Wednesday evening. Even though I was already tired, the adrenalin of excitement pumping in my muscles kept me going.

Papa and his youngest daughter MaryAnn who fished together, were first in the drift. When they finished with their drift, Allen and I followed as the second on the rotation. When Allen and I had finished throwing the net out and settled in for a drift, I looked around me. Because of the warm temperatures on that day, we didn't need parkas or rain jackets, and wore only light wool jackets over our sweaters. I thought of a trite cliché, worn out by some television beer commercial, "It doesn't get any better than this."

Allen offered me a chew, which I took, and after he pinched a dip into his lip, he tossed the empty can into the swirling water. I watched the can as it floated with us, rocking with us, turning like flotsam and jetsam from some oceanic accident. As the can spun past us and down the river, unencumbered as we were by a heavy net, I thought of the classic river metaphor of life. Where would the Copenhagen can finally end up? The Bering Sea? Where was my river of life taking me? I thought about the chance meeting of Allen and Clara at the Western Oregon Sate College nearly two years ago. How had that changed my life? How had I changed theirs? What would this trip to Alaska and knowing Allen, Clara, and their family mean for me in the future—miles down river? Like the Copenhagen can, I too faced a new and uncertain destination.

Drifting Yukon author, Dan Syljuberget, with a large chinook or king salmon.

I considered Allen and Clara with their traditional childhoods steeped in Yup'ik language and culture. I thought about how courageous they were to leave their home and travel to a college "outside"—as Alaska people refer to anywhere outside of Alaska—to work towards elementary education degrees with the goal of returning to their home in Yup'ik southwestern Alaska to help youth learn to comfortably walk in two or more worlds. They were passionate about cultural continuity with Yup'ik youth and about teaching them the Yup'ik language and culture while educating them to live in the modern macro culture.

Many years later, as I recalled this experience, it occurred to me for the first time ever that I too, with my experiences and passions, am a man who walks in multiple worlds. But really... what does that mean? What could I do with it, if anything, to be better in this world and for those around me?

Our first drift produced six kings and thirty chum. We'd have to do better than that to have a good season. By the fourth drift, our tote was quite full and the boat was heavy. We scanned the river for a fish collector. Earlier, Allen explained to me that fish collectors were larger boats that cruised up and down the river searching for independents, such as Allen, who had full totes and wanted to sell their catches. Since no fish collector was in sight, we motored back to camp. Once there, Allen called around on the CB radio, located in the kitchen tent, to locate a fish collector. The CB radio was the only means of communication between fish camps along the river. If news was needed to be passed up the river to Mountain Village or down the river to certain families, one simply got on the CB radio and called someone nearby in the direction the message needs to go. The person, in turn, relays the message to the next listener down on the line, and so on, until the message reaches its destination. The CB radio crackled with communication all the twenty-four hour day long. Sometimes we could hear four different languages in a single day: English, Yup'ik, Japanese, and Russian.

I found the way the Green family spoke on the CB radio very interesting. Without fail, Allen or Clyde would say "Yeah—okay—yeah" when giving an affirmative response to the person they communicated with on the other end of the CB radio, even if most of the conversation had been in Yup'ik. I started joking about this with Allen, and he didn't quite know what I was talking about until one day I prompted him to listen carefully to Clyde talking on the CB. When Clyde's conversation eventually came to a close, he said the inevitable, "Yeah—okay—yeah." Allen heard this and repeated it with a laugh. It would remain another item we would joke about throughout the summer.

Soon a message came back that a fish collector would be near our camp in a half-an-hour. As we cruised out to meet the fish collector, I noticed the sun was quite near the horizon. When we neared the much larger boat, Allen instructed me to grab a hold of it as we floated by and tie our boat to it. A huge dumpster-sized bucket attached to a boom swung over our boat. After we finished tossing our fish into the bucket, the captain of the fish collector boat read the scale attached to the boom-bucket apparatus. Typically the fish collector captain is a representative of a local cannery, and would crawl out of a boat cabin to punch holes in Allen's card for which he would later be paid by other cannery representatives. Sometimes, however, the fish collector may be a representative from a Japanese fishing ship settled somewhere outside of the mouth of the Yukon River and the Bering Sea. In these cases, Allen received cash, directly, for our catch.

While Allen and the captain settled their transaction, two deckhands unloaded the salmon into huge barrels and covered the fish with ice. I looked at the sun again—it was starting on its rise for the day. It had never set completely below the horizon. I had no clue as to the time. Here, there were only two instances where one needed to be concerned about the time: the 6:00 p.m. opening and closing times for each twenty-four hour period. It had been a slow opening for king season, according to Allen. Most commercial fishermen, including Allen, were angry with the Alaska Game and Fish for opening the season so late. By this late date, the bulk of the king salmon run had already passed.

We were all so tired when the period finally ended that we ate our supper in a zombie stupor while forcing our bodies to move. With a combination of a full belly and a long relaxing steam bath, sleep could no longer be avoided.

Chapter Twenty-seven
SUPERMAN IN GIRLS' SHOES

The Green family conversed most often in Yup'ik or a creolized combination of English and Yup'ik. Because I am monolingual, I often missed completely, or was the last to know about family decisions. Such was often the case when travel decisions were made. Usually the message would not get to me until shortly before departure often with a verbal warning less then five minutes before leaving. With these brief warnings, I had to prepare to leave in this very short time frame knowing fully that we might be gone to Mountain Village from camp for an entire week. I became very adept at preparing myself quickly for such trips. It did not take long, however, for me to learn to be like the Yup'ik Eskimo, to heighten my powers of observations and nonverbal communication, so that I knew well in advance that the family was preparing for a trip. What kept me guessing was exactly when we'd be leaving. The morning after our first commercial fishing period, I remembered Clara giving extra portions of old dry fish to the dogs and noted this as a sure sign of a shortly upcoming trip.

Then Allen informed me that we'd be going to Mountain Village for supplies, especially water and more barrels of gasoline.

We spent several days at Mountain Village and were preparing to leave to return to fish camp. It was going to be a long, long day because as soon as we would get to camp, we'd have to quickly prepare for the next commercial fishing period which would start at 6:00 p.m. that evening. I lay on the beach below the store "guarding" the boat while the others shopped at the village store. Allen and I had spent the morning dragging two foot by twelve foot old scrap boards down the hill to put into the boat. We planned to make bunk-beds and an outhouse. I laid there with my head on a piece of driftwood just thinking. I had my hat pulled down over my eyes and glasses so I could relax better. In the sunshaded darkness, I could see reflections in my glass lenses of the frames of my glasses, and some of my hairs. They looked huge—like looking through a microscope. Then I heard a young voice, startling me from my introspection.

"Look at that man wearing funny girls' shoes."

Tired of working in my sweaty and clumsy rubber knee high boots, I had switched to my Birkenstock sandals. I took off my hat, turned over on my left shoulder and squinted at three little girls. I located the speaker, a chubby little girl with a dirty white T-shirt, torn black knit pants, and black rubber knee high boots—the kind with a red strip around the top. She came forward, obviously the fearless one of the trio. "Do you know what it says on the back of my necklace?"

I got up to look at her necklace. "Made in Mexico," I read while noticing her long black hair and big ears that bend at the tips. She was six years old, I learned, and her two-half sisters, five and seven.

"Aren't you that guy everyone calls 'Superman'?"

I laughed "yes" and remembered a trio of boys in the village, who were about the same age as these girls. For some strange reason, the boys always shouted, "Superman" whenever I walked by. My hair was considerably thinner on top than that of "Superman" actor Christopher Reeves and I always wear a hat when outside. I am much hairier about the face than the actor. To this day I still don't understand why I reminded them of the "Superman" movies that were recently playing on the old movie channel.

As I stood there remembering the actor and the "Superman" movie, an old Yup'ik woman trudged up the gravel road to the store. She wore a summer-weight woman's kuspac, an old scarf of indeterminate color over her head, and a pair of old, faded red polyester socks pulled up tight around her skinny calves. On her feet, she wore a pair of cheap imitation running shoes, the kind you'd find at Shopko or Kmart. They were probably bought at the village store. I looked back from the ancient face walking on by and then looked back to my three new little friends. They played a little game of scaring each other with bugs; the scared ones scooted behind my legs grabbing them in the process. As I stood there quietly and watched them play about me, I wondered what their destinies will be like. What changes would come to the Yuk'ip people?

Chapter Twenty-eight

YUKON FISHING WARS

We arrived at camp right at 6:00 p.m., the opening time for commercial fishing periods. Everyone scurried like frenzied squirrels to unload the scrap lumber and supplies from the boats to camp. It was a mad rush, grabbing rain pants, rubber-knee-high boots, locating fishing gloves, and loading nets and totes into the boat. Allen bellowed at me, "Get the permits! Get my coat! And snuff!"

Allen seemed to be in a cranky mood. I did not feel much better because I thought we should have traveled back to camp yesterday and therefore would have been able to take our time unloading the boats and preparing for this fishing period.

I knew Allen was impatient when we didn't wait for our turn to drift; instead, we drove over to the far side of the river, where nobody fished. Allen wanted to fish there while Leonard completed his drift in the well-established drifting spot. Shortly after we let our net out we had to pull it in because of numerous snags. It was tremendously hard work, to pull in the net loaded as it was with logs and tree branches. One branch was so tangled that it seemed to take nearly a half-an-hour to remove it from the net. Such fishing conditions were risky as snags could ruin $1000 nets.

In the time I worked with Allen that summer, I developed a deep appreciation of his knowledge of boats, his ability to read the river, and to predict the actions of the fish and other animals of this tundra-river ecosystem. But on that particular day, I was not pleased with Allen. His hurry-up-and-wait attitude and blind stubbornness of that particular fishing period only added fuel to the fire. The situation at hand, however, never erupted into a fight between us even though we snapped at each other often throughout the entire twenty-four hour period.

Allen Green on the left and author nearest to the boat are getting ready to go for a drift. Note the large plastic tote in the boat to collect fish an♦ the large ball in the bow of the boat. That is the float for the net. The lower Yukon River is the back♦rop.

We drifted three times in that snag-riddled area and only had five kings and a small number of chums to show for it. Meanwhile, Leonard had twenty-nine kings and a large number of chums after only one drift in the usual spot just beyond the big sandbar. That spot had been fished so often that most of the nasty snags were cleaned out long ago. Leonard hollered at us when he came back from his drift that he was going in to eat while the others took their turns drifting. We hadn't eaten since morning so the idea of Leonard having a good drift and going in to eat made both Allen and me even crankier with each other.

Typically, we spent the first third of each period rushing around here and there fishing for the mystical mother lode of the king run. Because of this excursion, we lost three or four turns at the tried and tested drifting spot while Allen's brothers, Leonard and Clyde each were netting more fish than we were. After only three drifts, Leonard's total was fifty-five kings. He decided to sleep for a few hours and then drift later. We had only eleven kings after eight drifts. We fished non-stop for the entire period to bag fifty-nine kings (they did not count the chum). The number of kings caught determines the success of the fishing period.

Even though I was frustrated with Allen, I never mentioned anything about sticking to the traditional spot. I still felt like a left-handed monkey driving the kicker and a blind baboon throwing the net out. Besides, Allen was my friend and this was just a bad day. He didn't say anything in anger to me either. He knew me well, liked me, and wanted to understand my moods just as well as I strove to understand his.

About midnight, we finally began drifts in the traditional spot when we encountered a trespasser. It was still light out. The rest of the Green family was sleeping. Behind me and our tote, Allen sat stock straight on his butt board with black pupils blazing in the dimming light, and an easy hand on the familiar throttle-handle of smaller kicker. Ahead of me, across about seventy-five feet of water, was the intruder sticking his hairy face out of the window of his boat cabin which protected both him and his displayed shotgun from the rain.

"You better get the fuck outa here!" Allen stood up in our boat, braced his stocky legs against the butt-board between them and leaned over the rear of the boat to spit his two-hour old snuff dip into the swirling water fighting the steady blades of the idling kicker. "No one can fish here! This is our fishing ground! Go find your own fucking spot."

"No one owns the river! I'll set (my net) here if I want to!"

I remained seated and silent, perhaps a little embarrassed at the confrontation. I was surprised at Allen's language and anger. I had never known him to use the word "fuck" or any other swear word for that matter in his speech except during those times in which he was drunk and violent. But he had left those days far behind him now. Allen was dead sober now and had been for some time. With a quiet inner strength, he had beaten alcoholism. Now he was fighting for an unwritten life-right to fish his family waters.

Our opponent, the white man of a cabined boat, cursed back at Allen quoting Alaska commercial fishing regulations which allowed anyone owning a Zone Y-1 fishing permission to fish anywhere in the Zone Y-1 fishing district.

"My family was fishing this spot before you were born! It is ours—it has been for centuries. You better not set your fucking net here."

"God dammit! I will if I want to!"

Up to this point, I had my own private battle swirling inside of me. Looking at the white man's shotgun, I wondered whether I should be scared of this tense situation or succumb to an untimely urge to break out laughing. It reminded me of a

Author on a drift on the Yukon River, prior to pulling on rain pants to wear while pulling in the net.

typical scene in a high school baseball game in which a strutting, nervous batter and a cocky, teasing catcher get into a verbal fight, perhaps even in a petty brawl.

There was a possibility that our situation here could turn into a physical act. Suddenly, I was acutely aware of my position. All humor was dissolved. All my senses became very alert and tuned. I was in a direct line between the white man and Allen. A pair of pintails whistled overhead. Upriver a droning fish collector engine could be heard. Allen slapped a bloody mosquito on his face and brushed off her lifeless body. The white-man glared back in our direction.

Finally, I stood up, not really thinking why, knowing that it wasn't my fight and knowing I wouldn't speak because I was not in a position to do so. On my left stood my closest friend, a Yup'ik Eskimo, braced to defend his claim to a family fishing ground, a writ of the ancient land. On my right was the enemy, the white-man, the "kass'aq," with a factory-made boat, his weaponry, and the laws of paper, courts, and modern "civilized society."

All was quiet now, except for the low idling of a pair of kicker motors. As I stood, I turned to face the intruder for the first time. Conscious that I was exposing my incriminating whiskered face and obviously Caucasian height to him, I took my stand and stared back at him with my pale white-man eyes. His blue eyes flickered momentarily with a mixture of surprise and loathing and then he looked away.

Allen ordered me to throw out our net for setting as we slowly turned from the intruder. As I did so, my back felt exposed, and I could feel the intruder's eyes, shotgun pellets of hatred, piercing right through my rain slicker, wool sweater, long underwear, and into my naked skin. After we set the net, the white-man sped away.

Around 8:00 a.m., it started to rain. The temperature must have been above freezing, but it seemed colder than that with the rain and wind. Allen and I were totally exhausted—just drained. Every effort exerted for the remaining ten hours was done through sheer willpower. We just willed ourselves to push the boat out to the deeper water—get in, throw the net out, and will ourselves to have the energy to pull the net in when the drift was done.

Around noon we pulled ashore for breakfast. Exhausted, we stumbled out of the boat, tripped over each other while stumbling out of our rain pants, and dragged ourselves into the kitchen. There we found Clara and Ma in the process of making pancakes on the little kitchen wood stove.

I struggled through the fatigue, while eating breakfast. It seemed that in the crowded conditions, people were eating right on top of each other. The sense of claustrophobia always present in the kitchen tent was overpowering when in an extreme state of exhaustion. I took off my glasses to rub my eyes. When I opened them, a well-rested, spirited little kid had grabbed them. While I was in the process of recovering my stolen glasses, another kid swiped my pancakes. I grabbed some toilet paper and headed for the trees so tired that I could barely swat the clouds of mosquitoes following me.

Little Lucy followed me. Donnie followed her while performing his favorite sport of making her cry. She screamed bloody hell. Donnie mentioned to me glee-fully, "Let's just leave her." After taking Lucy back to the kitchen tent, I resumed my journey into the trees. I tried to go—but no go—I was just too pooped to poop. The mosquitoes scored again on my spotted ass. I stuck the roll of toilet paper into the pocket of my kuspac for future use, and scratching my butt, hoped that I would be able to wash my wool long-johns soon so that at least I'd have clean underwear rubbing on my mosquito bites.

"Dan. Come!"

Another drift to be made. Oh sleep, beautiful sleep.

Chapter Twenty-nine
BERRY PICKING ON THE TUNDRA

Several weeks after the Yukon Fishing Wars incident and on our final period of the king salmon commercial fishing season, Allen and I straggled exhausted into the kitchen tent, empty of people at about 5:00 a.m. for a snack. After eating, Allen threw his coat down on the ground in a corner of the tent, curled up on it and promptly fell asleep. I laid back on the picnic table bench on which I was seated and also fell asleep. I awoke sometime later to find the kitchen tent noisy and bustling with people. Allen and I had been asleep for a few hours. Several people from a nearby fish collector boat were drinking coffee. One of them gestured in my direction, "He snores."

When I stood up, my left knee, still asleep, gave away and I fell on top of Allen causing him to awake with a start. The nap served us well for after a gargantuan breakfast, we left the kitchen tent as refreshed as ever and were able to fish the remaining seven hours of the period in good spirits. It is amazing how just a few hours of sleep can rejuvenate the body.

The next day, I learned the hard way, not to hang up my wet socks to dry in the fish house.

Almost everyone hung their wet clothing to dry around the small cast-iron wood-burning stove in the kitchen tent. Often, with many other articles of clothing hanging to dry, there wasn't enough room to hang my wet garments. I decided on that fateful day to hang my socks in the fish house where a nice fire was drying the fish. I was careful to hang them well away from the open fire so that they would not burn, and well away from the fish so that the strips would not be contaminated by my stinking foot odor and perspiration. While hanging my socks, I wondered why no one else had considered the nifty idea of using the fish house as a place to dry wet clothing. Several hours later, I was eating a lunch of salmon stew in the kitchen tent with Allen and Papa, when Clara burst into the tent bellowing, "Who put their socks in the fish house?"

"I did. What's wrong Clara?"

She replied with great animation of hands and facial expressions, "We never, never, EVER, never put clothing in the fish house!"

Papa Green added in his broken English, "No clothing in fish house."

When I asked "why", Clara repeated her "never, never" speech. I failed to receive an explanation. At first I thought that they were concerned that my socks would contaminate the fish. But after looking around the inside of the kitchen tent and noticing wet and drying socks, gloves, hats, and jeans hanging in such close proximity to open bags of potato chips, rice, and Sailor-Boy-Pilot-Bread crackers that clothing and food practically touched, this thought was immediately dismissed. It wasn't until later, back in Oregon that I learned, while reading a book on Yup'ik Eskimo culture, that the Yup'iks have a tremendous respect for the subsistence they reap from nature. The act of hanging my dirty, soggy, stinky socks in a shed of drying salmon strips was an act of disrespect to the salmon. The Yup'ik Eskimos have humility in their approach to nature. Without the harvesting of salmon, both for the purpose of selling to commercial buyers and for winter subsistence in the form of dry-fish, they may not be able to survive. Yet, they have survived in a very harsh climate for millennia mostly because they approached nature with humility and respect. As I trekked out to the fish house to gather my socks, Clara hollered, "Dan...look for buckets. We leave for berry picking soon."

We gathered containers of all sizes, and river travel-clothing for the berry-picking adventure. Clara asked Clyde to bring a rifle in case a bear became interested in us. Allen located his huge kite bought at the Oregon coast. When I asked him why he was bringing it, he replied, "You'll see."

Allen drove us across the river from camp to the opposite shore and then roughly two miles downriver. He eased us into a small cove from which rose a sandy bank about twenty yards to the tundra. Even though the bank was very steep, we had little trouble climbing it. We just dug footholds into the sandy soil. Soon all of us, Papa Joseph, Allen, Clyde, Clara, MaryAnn, Mike, Donnie, Jimmy, and I were on the tundra searching for delicious salmonberries.

The tundra—often thought of as a barren wasteland mostly due to a scarcity of trees—was anything but barren. All vegetation was very close to the ground. The tallest plants, including the salmonberry plant, reached only inches above the surface of the tundra.

Walking on the tundra was a unique experience in itself for I sunk down a mushy three to six inches with each step I took. Under my rubber-booted foot was layer upon layer of compacted lichen and mosses. I dug with my hand down through the fragile tundra surface to a depth of about twelve inches and failed to find soil. We all wore rubber knee high boots, which were a necessity as the low places on the tundra were marshy and boggy. The rainwater could seep only so far through the layers of mosses and lichens before it stopped at the permafrost soil.

Once we reached the top of the bank and were on the tundra, Allen unrolled his giant Oregon coast kite, assembled it, and soon had it airborne without taking a step. The Alaska wind was strong enough that he just simply let it take the kite out into the sky. After staking the kite's string-reel to the tundra, he explained, "Now when we scatter out on the tundra, we'll always know where the boat is because the kite is flying above it." Looking down the steep bank to the boat anchored some thirty yards below on the beach, I realized the simple genius of the idea for there was no way we'd be able to see the boat when we stepped even a few steps back from the edge of the bank.

We casually split into two groups. Allen and I had been together constantly since we arrived from Oregon and we needed a break from each other. I wanted to get to know his father, Joseph, so I joined Clara, MaryAnn, and Papa Joseph who had a two-way radio tucked in the pocket of his kuspac. The boys, Donnie, Jimmy, and Mike followed Clyde and Allen, who had the other two-way radio. We were all armed with various containers and each group had a five gallon plastic bucket. Our two groups could not stray too far from each other as only Clyde carried his 30.06 rifle as a bear deterrent. We all wore kuspacs with the hoods drawn tightly around our faces and gloves to protect us from the droves of mosquitoes rising up from the bogs on the tundra.

The salmonberry looked very similar to the blackberries I had picked in Oregon. It was a tightly compacted bundle of small juicy globes. Unlike the ripe blackberry, however, which was very dark purple, the salmonberry was a very light orange-peach in color. Not nearly as delicious as the Oregon blackberry, which shot the taste-buds with memorable sweetness, the salmonberry, while blander in taste, was nevertheless quite tasty. One could taste the smells of the tundra when eating an Alaskan salmonberry. The Green family spent many summer hours picking them to freeze for food during the winter months when fresh fruit flown into the community from the "outside" is scarce.

After several hours of berry picking, my juice pitcher was full of plump salmon berries. I looked around for Papa Joseph, who had a five-gallon plastic bucket with him. He was seated on the tundra beside the bucket, just smoking Marlboros and watching. Never knowing how to converse with him because of our totally different cultural backgrounds, especially his limited knowledge of English language combined with my total lack of understanding of the Yup'ik language, I nevertheless was curious about the elderly Eskimo man who had seen tremendous changes in his lifetime. As I strode over to him, the best I could come up with to say to him, however, stretching my legs from one clump of compacted lichens and mosses to another, was a generic, "How ya doin', Papa?"

"Good." He breathed heavily while he smoked. He watched. I sat down on the tundra beside him and decided I would learn more by listening and watching than talking. So I too listened and watched.

I remembered observing Papa helping with chores around camp. He seemed to possess substantial physical strength despite his frail, old appearance. Although he was about five feet two inches tall with very bowed, arthritic, and spindly legs, I watched him time after time hoist a heavy log over one shoulder and shuffle over to the saw horses to chainsaw it into pieces for splitting, all the while whistling an odd tuneless breathy song in time to his deliberate steps.

I remained quiet just watching the tundra with Papa while observing him out of the corner of my eye. Sharing the moment quietly with him seemed to be more respectful and meaningful than filling the air with questions and other chatter. Culturally traditional Yup'iks, such as Papa Joseph, watch and listen. Then they act.

After a while of viewing the tundra, Papa Joseph dug into his kuspac pocket and pulled out his two-way radio. He lengthened the antenna, spoke Yup'ik phrases into it, and waited for a response. Allen's voice crackled Yup'ik words through Papa's two-way radio. The conversation was short. And afterwards, Papa closed the antenna, stuffed the unit back into his kuspac pocket, struggled to his feet, and said simply, "We go."

I silently followed. My Anglo upbringing in South Dakota and Oregon, a macro culture of automobiles, retail stores, and restaurants seemed remote and distant from my past. The Yup'ik way-of-life, including gathering food from nature, such as salmon fishing and berry picking felt present, important, and real. As I carefully picked my way from one clump of vegetation to the other and closely watching the path of Papa, I felt like I had one foot in one world and the other in another world. My roots as the eldest son of a men's clothier and a college professor, born and raised in South Dakota to age sixteen seemed to fade with each step. Even images of college life at WOSC seemed remote and irrelevant. I was dressed in the summer attire of an adult Yup'ik male. I was honored with a Yup'ik name, by a Yup'ik elder, a very rare occurrence, especially as the name given to me was after a much-revered Yup'ik hunter and wise-man from the past. I had stood and faced down a white intruder who legally had the right to fish the Green family's traditional drifting spot. Just the previous day, a Yup'ik visitor to our camp confused me as being the young brother of Allen and Clyde, despite my beard and build. Again, I felt like I was walking in two worlds.

Several weeks later, after Allen paid me for the first part of the commercial season, Joseph had more to say to me. With a broad smile and black eyes twinkling with an odd mixture of merriment and sadness, he said, "Dan. When you go outside, you buy big case of whiskey with fish money and get really drunk like Eskimo." Then he gave a hearty chuckle; his whole body shook with laughter. When his laughing ceased, he looked sadly down towards the ground.

Four years later, "Papa" Joseph Green died of lung cancer at the age of seventy-four. He left me with the lasting impression as a man who was physically and spiritually closer to nature than anyone I have ever known.

Chapter Thirty
BREAK AT MOUNTAIN VILLAGE

The king salmon season had closed and all fishing would be illegal for a week or two until the Alaska State Fish and Game opened commercial fishing again. No longer would king nets with the eight and three-quarter inch mesh be legal until king season rolled around next summer. For the remainder of this summer, fishing would be legal only with nets having five and seven-eighths inch mesh. Anyone caught fishing with a king net would be served a stiff fine. The break served as a time to buy new supplies, do some hunting and sport-fishing, more berry-picking, and a time to relax for a while. For me, the break meant some time for getting caught up on my letter writing. For the others, it meant getting caught up on the village gossip. More importantly, the Green family had to attend a funeral of a relative in Pilot Station, about fifty miles upriver from Mountain Village. I wondered if I would be going too.

While we traveled up the Yukon from camp toward Mountain Village, we came upon a full-grown moose swimming across the channel. She passed right in front of the boat. We could have touched her with an oar as we throttled slowly past her. We were near Mountain Village in the smaller calmer fork of the river, the channel around the long island just downriver from Mountain Village. The magnificent cow was crossing over to the island. I wondered if a full-grown healthy moose, such as this one, would be successful in an attempt to cross the main channel of the river on the other side of the island where the water is deep, wide, and swift.

Allen and I had decided together privately that I would not be going to the funeral with the rest of the family to help economize room in Allen's boat.

Everyone went to the funeral in Pilot Station except Clyde, Leonard, and me. Before leaving, Allen gave me instructions not to play the television or stereo too loud in the evening, and to not answer the door for any reason as there were a lot of drunks stumbling around. Allen's oldest brother, Leonard, who lived by himself in the older home down on the bank of the Yukon did not go with the family to Pilot Station as he had a court date in St. Mary's. He had been arrested for public drunkenness and disorderly conduct earlier in the spring.

The morning after the family left for Pilot Station, Clyde, and I got up about 11:00 a.m., drank coffee, and watched a movie until about one. We ate some left-over salmon, gathered a shotgun, a handful of shotgun shells, some sport fishing gear, and headed over to Clearwater Sloughs. Clearwater got its local name by contrasting its crystal clear water—sometimes you can see fifteen feet down—to the murky, silt-laden waters of the Yukon. The sloughs were a menagerie of rivers, streams, ponds, and lakes that all eventually drain into the Yukon. These waters are host to one of the most prolific and important breeding grounds for North American waterfowl. The waters abound with varieties of fish ranging from northern pike to salmon entering them from the Yukon searching for their birthplace in order to spawn. Beaver and muskrat are also plentiful in these waters.

We accidentally encountered Ellen, a sister of Allen and Clyde's, and mother of Jimmy and Mike, rod-and-reel fishing with her common-law husband, Irvin. They had a boatful of kids, including Donnie, Jimmy, and Mike; all three boys crawled over to our boat. The mosquitoes were getting vicious, biting through everything, so Clyde decided we'd head back to the more open and windier Yukon. Once onto the Yukon, however, the boys talked Clyde into heading over the sloughs on the other side of the river for some beaver hunting.

Chapter Thirty-One
TWO DEAD BIRDS

Several hours later, while scratching my privates where a naughty mosquito had managed to penetrate my jeans, I felt relief that we were finally traveling back to Mountain Village at the end the day. My butt was sore from bouncing on the wooden board in the boat and I was tired of being the recipient of the mischievous antics of the three spoiled boys. We were cruising toward the Yukon on a small stream where, a half-hour earlier, Donnie had missed shooting a quiet beaver. The boys were hungry for a kill.

Nearing the entrance to the Yukon, a large male whistler swan bolted elegantly out of some rushes and into the evening air.

"Shoot it!" the cousins yelled to Clyde who swung his care-neglected rusted Remington pump through the swan's flight.

The swan absorbed the hurt shock and dropped with the long graceful neck looped horribly into the rushes. It struggled and managed to ascend to flight again. This time it landed about fifty yards ahead of us and swam desperately as it was dying, with its neck wobbling horribly back and forth and side to side.

"It's drunk," the boys laughed as Clyde fumbled with his gun and yellow twenty-gauge shells.

While closing my eyes to shut out the scene, I remembered a hot South Dakota summer day, two fifteen-year old boys, and a .22 rifle. I had taken my friend, Mark, out shooting. After several hours of plinking at cans, we saw an owl just kind of loping along slowly through the air. Mark, who held the little rifle, asked, "Should I shoot at it?" Thinking he would miss, I told him to go ahead.

After he took aim at the flying owl, the rifle wavering unsteadily, he shot. The little owl folded into a tight ball, fell to the dirt, making a muffled "prff" as he hit.

When we walked up to him, he was lying on his back. His eyes were staring straight back at us with a pained, questioning look of "why?" Then he relaxed. He looked like a beautiful and special bird of nature. Now he was dead. Mark finally broke the silence in a slow-hushed voice, "Gee, I didn't think I'd hit him."

I looked back at the swan still struggling in the water as we pulled up next to it. The boys excitedly pulled it in. I grabbed it to wring its neck to shorten its misery, but soon found neck-wringing does not work effectively with long-necked birds. Looking at it dying on the floor of the boat, Clyde spoke quietly to me, "I shouldn't have shot it. They're mating now." Then he added, "But it will be a good change of diet from salmon."

two dead birds

oh we were young and tough one summer, remember?
that owl was still and quiet, but yet we shot
looked we, then dead on the dirt—a nature member
what aim have we to slay; what's been forgot?

The riverman swung boat to enter the slough
warm swan ascends to air, absorbs hurt shock
came down with twist of neck into the cold blue
then sway from right to left, one less from flock

two boys, a man, a swan, one lonely owl
one death fulfills the expectations of a duo
one life forfeits to feed another's bowel
that nature's grace ends nonchalant, where wrought that
rule?

the pleasure hunt of man for bird
without the gun its shot's still heard

Dan Syljuberget

Chapter Thirty-two
ALCOHOL, DEATH, AND FEAR

As Clyde and I walked back up to the house after beaching his boat, we passed three boys about eighteen years old that were sharing a bottle of bootleg whiskey. One of the boys was so drunk he could barely stand up while the other two cursed at the top of their lungs at everyone who passed by. It was going to be a wild weekend. There were a lot of people in town during this break in the commercial fishing seasons.

We arrived at the house about 1:30 a.m., ate a little and went to bed around 3:00 a.m. When we got up the next day, Clyde wanted to go to Pilot Station. I didn't want to go; I wanted to get caught up on some letter writing and to be alone for a while. Besides, Allen and I had agreed prior that it would likely be very crowded at the Green's relative's home in Pilot Station. So Clyde found his cousin, Sam Green, to travel with him. Since both were heavy drinkers, I wondered if they would get to Pilot Station.

Allen surprised me by coming through the door around 6:00 p.m. He was very tense. He and a cousin had been dragging the river for a body between Pilot Station and Saint Mary's. They slept four hours that morning at his cousin's home in Saint Mary's with no success. William had boated downriver to Mountain Village for a few supplies. Apparently a man's boat had washed up on the shore near Pilot Station with no one in it. The man, who hadn't been seen for several days, had last been seen drinking with several others. No corpse was ever found. The man had simply disappeared.

Allen helped dig four graves in Mountain Village that summer; all four deaths were alcohol related. Allen said the drinking had been very heavy those last two nights in Pilot Station, and he expected the same in Mountain Village. He added that the drinking in the village would get worse over the summer before it got better. "A friend of mine in Pilot Station told me that he was sick of it and was going to move."

The funeral of Allen's relative in Pilot Station had been moved to Monday. As he left to head back to Pilot Station, Allen again warned me not to unlock the door, to play the stereo or TV with low volume, and to not answer the door if someone knocks on it. I had the feeling when he left that he had just stopped in to see how I was doing. There were stores in St. Mary's where he could have purchased his supplies.

That evening, Leonard, Allen's oldest brother, called to see if I was okay. He said, "There's a lot of crazy drunks running around—don't go outside." He gave me his number and that of the Public Safety Office. Before he hung up, he said, "Try to be quiet, Dan, but leave the lights on. Anyone will just come in if they think there is a party. Or try to break in looking for booze money if they think there is a party. Clyde never arrived in Pilot Station," he quietly added.

Shortly after he hung up, I heard footsteps on the outside porch. It sounded like a shuffle between two people intermingled with an occasional curse. Then a very loud single bang on the door. I waited quietly and heard the people stumble off the steps and move away from the house. I looked at the clock—1:00 a.m.— still some light out. ATVs bumped up and down the graveled roads. I heard the people shouting, screaming, laughing crazily, and cursing. I peeked out the kitchen window and spotted two men trying to walk down the path behind the houses. One got tangled up in a clothesline scattering laundry everywhere. The two men struggled to their feet and continued to stagger along their journey. A lot of money flowed around town with people receiving payouts from the cannery for their salmon harvest during the break in the commercial seasons. There was a lot of booze flowing in town as well.

I cooked the dog salmon left for me and ate it along with some homemade bread. I heard gunshots. I turned a tape of Paul McCartney's *Pipes of Peace* on the stereo.

More gunshots. Feeling rather silly, I checked both doors again to see if they were locked and wedged a chair under the door knob of both doors.

More drunken screaming. More crazy laughter.

I sat down. My fear slowly turning to anger. Why do people live like this— don't they care? I remember Ma Green remarking about Monmouth, Oregon, when they came down for Clara's graduation, "It sure is nice to be in a place where you don't have to worry about crazy drunks running around." I became really mad remembering her statement and scrambled around for something to use as a club. Any damn asshole that breaks in here is going to get it in the teeth!

Sheesh. Boy am I tough! I sat down to listen to McCartney again. Restlessly, I turned it off. I turned on the TV. As I observed a big gunfight during the old John Wayne movie, *Rio Bravo*, I remembered the McCartney album I played earlier. Reflecting on this, I recalled an old Beatles song, "All we are saying—is give peace a chance." I think Lennon was the lead singer. I went to bed feeling like a fool for getting hostile.

Chapter Thirty-three

THE FAMILY RETURNS

Toward evening of the next day, the Green family returned from Pilot Station. We all lounged around watching TV and talking. Allen told me privately that it was a good thing that I had not gone along because it got very crowded.

It was getting late when Clyde stumbled drunk through the doors. More interesting than Clyde's state of inebriation was the family's reaction. Everyone quietly headed towards their respective bedrooms and closed the doors. Everyone, that is, except Allen, Clyde, and me. We sat for a while listening to Clyde's drunken tales of fighting in Vietnam. Clyde had never been to Vietnam, but his older brothers had. He had never traveled anyplace outside of Alaska, except to Oregon. However that point seemed minor at the moment. When he seemed to have calmed somewhat, Allen and I went to our beds. A few minutes after we were in our bedrooms, we heard a loud crash followed by curses. When Clyde was around, he slept out in the hide-a-bed couch in the living room. Clyde had tipped over a lamp. I heard Allen exit his room and go over to Clyde.

"This is not your house, Clyde. This is Mom and Pop's house. You can't be breaking things and acting like a fool here. Now quiet down and go to bed."

After several minutes of the two brothers arguing—Allen trying to calm Clyde down and Clyde being belligerent—Clyde finally settled into bed. Perhaps Clyde knew, even in his drunken state, that his younger, stronger brother could have manhandled him into settling down.

When I padded out of the bedroom the next morning and into the kitchen, Ma was seated with a big mixing bowl supported between an arm and a pajamaed thigh. With her other bare hand, she stirred and kneaded a dough-like mixture in the bowl. It looked like there were berries mixed in with the dough.

Yawning and stretching, I sleepily asked, "Whatcha got there, Ma, dough?"

She laughed heartily with her whole body shaking as she turned to Clara who was making pancakes. "Clara, he thinks it's dough." Clara looked back at me with her black eyes twinkling. Ma explained, "It's fish. We're making akutuk, Eskimo ice cream. Cooked and boned fish mixed with Crisco lard, and squeezed berries."

Clara added, "You'll like it, Dan."

Later, I sampled some. It didn't taste like fish at all. It was very cold because of the ice and I could taste the berries. I imagined "akutuk" to be a very nutritious dish. A combination of a new morning and with hominess of Ma and Clara's cooking brought a much needed peace from the tense and violent previous couple of days. Things seem to have returned to some normalcy and balance.

Chapter Thirty-four

KIDS

Yup'ik Eskimo children are basically spoiled and receive little discipline unless it is to prevent them from doing something dangerous or destructive. As the only white man they had ever had direct contact with or had personally gotten to know (aside from Donnie's experiences living in Oregon with his mother, Clara), I received varying degrees of attention from the Green kids ranging from wonder at the skinny, balding, and bearded, white man early on to later being the recipient of childish practical jokes.

Donnie Green on cold wet travel day.

Lucy and her grandmother, Arlene Green, in the kitchen tent.

My beard, in particular, fascinated the children. They had all seen bearded white men previously but never up close. Once in close contact with me, a strong tactile sense overcame any shyness they may have had initially. By the end of the summer, my beard had grown long and bushy and the little girls, IdaMae, Lizzy, and Lucy all liked to sit on my lap and stroke my beard.

But it was Mike who first put beard-wonder into words. One time we were all lounging around in the camp kitchen tent during a rainstorm. Mike was sitting on my lap while we were reading an Archie comic book. Mike grew bored with Archie and reached up to stroke my beard. "Ah—ah—feel like rug. Donnie come feel!" Soon all of the children had to come feel Dan's beard.

Little two-year old Lucy, in particular, took a liking to me. I was "my Dan" to her, and she'd loudly proclaim this to everyone present whenever she'd spy me.

Lucy had a unique, if not painful way of showing affection—biting. She would sneak up on me and without warning, I'd feel a sharp pain in my leg or arm, and there removing her little fangs from flesh would be Lucy flashing a toothy grin.

One time in a state of extreme exhaustion during a commercial fishing period, I lost my patience with her oral attraction to me. After she released her tooth grip on my arm, I chomped on her finger. She let out an unearthly scream and backed away from me – eyeing me with surprise and anger. She screamed for so long and was so loud that I felt a little guilty, but Ma, Lucy's grandmother, scolded her, "You shouldn't be biting Dan. Now you know it hurts." For about a week, Lucy avoided me like I was a two-headed monster. During that time, I was no longer "my Dan," but she never bit me again.

Several weeks after I bit Lucy, torrential rains and winds again confined us to the tiny cabins and the kitchen tent at fish camp. We lounged around reading, talking, and listening to the weather outside. We were all very bored and feeling cabin-fever with twelve of us holed up in the larger cabin. Suddenly there came a pronounced pungent odor. MaryAnn peered down the back of Lucy's diaper and declared, "Oh Lucy, you smell bad."

Changing Lucy's diaper in the small confines of the sixteen-by-sixteen foot cabin in the midst of twelve people was quite an olfactory experience for all. The strong odor in such a tiny cabin just about reeled us over. The young boys groaned loudly, "Oh Lucy, you stink." The air was so putrid that I thought I was going to vomit. Clyde quietly exited the cabin to brave the pouring rain to the kitchen tent. As her mother scrambled for a fresh diaper, Lucy lay on her back with her naked butt in the air wiggling her fat little legs. She giggled impishly and gleefully commanded, "My Dan – come smell me!" I was "my Dan" again.

Chapter Thirty-five
ALONE WITH CLYDE AT CAMP

The Green family needed to make a quick supply run from fish camp to Mountain Village. Because the drying fish were hung in the fish house and the fire needed to be kept burning continually, Clyde and I elected to stay at camp while the others headed to Mountain Village in Allen's boat. Camp seemed quiet without the activity of boisterous kids.

After several hours, Clyde declared, "Let's go see if there are any fish in the river; we don't have much anything to eat."

As we let the net out, Clyde mentioned that we might not have any luck as the salmon were between runs. The Yukon could be relatively void of fish except for the occasional stragglers. After several drifts that did not yield a single fish, Clyde suggested we pull in and go hunting. Once back to camp, we located the rusty twenty-gauge pump shotgun and a couple of shells. In less than five minutes, we were again on the water and heading across the Yukon toward the sloughs and streams which fed the river.

As Clyde and I wound our way through the wilderness menagerie of nameless sloughs, streams, ponds, and lakes that teemed with wildlife and eventually fed into the Yukon, I was struck again, as I was when we cruised similar waters near Mountain Village, of the raw, unique beauty of this place. When people think of beautiful wilderness areas, typically images that come to mind are snow-capped mountains and lush green forests. The Yukon delta region with its many waters interspersed with rolling tundra of low growing vegetation had neither snow-capped mountains nor lush-green forests, yet it has a raw, pristine quality of its own.

We were cruising along a stream, peering ahead to spot ducks and wondering what new sight was around each bend, when Clyde suddenly slowed the boat and idled it up to an enormous mound of willow branches and twigs on the bank of the stream. The mound led down into the water. It was as nearly as large as a single stall car garage.

"Do you know what that is, Dan?"

"No…what is it?"

"It's a beaver house—one of the biggest I've ever seen."

I was thoroughly enjoying Clyde's company. In town he was constantly edgy, always itching for a drink, but away from Mountain Village and its temptations and at fish camp, he was quiet, reflective, and peaceful. He really enjoyed nature and didn't rush through it like his brothers did. As the saying goes, "He stops to smell the roses." Hungry as we were, Clyde proved this by stopping to examine a beaver house.

Several bends on the stream later we approached a trio of mallards. Clyde rose quickly from his seat, pointed the well-worn Remington and shot once. A drake fell. It was all we needed for supper.

Chapter Thirty-six
WINDING DOWN
AND GOODBYE

It was the second week of August and near the end of the silver (Coho) salmon commercial season, the last commercial fishing season for the year. The "silver season" was much more relaxed than the "king season" in June. For kings, we fished for twenty-four hour periods. For silvers, we could only legally fish for twelve hour periods. We had time for berry picking, hunting, and exploring the sloughs and streams. We made a trip downriver to a tiny village, just a scant few miles from the mouth of the Yukon at the Bering Sea, to purchase supplies at an ancient and rustic store.

But now was time for me to return to Oregon. I had told my family that I would be returning home around the middle of August. Allen urged me to stay another week so that I could go moose hunting with him. I often regret that I hadn't stayed for the experience. However, I had several things that I needed to do before school started. Mike, my brother, was moving back to Corvallis to start school again at OSU, my parents had separated, and I needed to look for a place to live in Monmouth. Throughout the course of the summer, I decided that I was going to change my major from Elementary Education to Secondary Education and Language Arts. Learning about English language usage and the writing process seemed much more interesting to me than being an elementary teacher. All of these details needed my attention during the few weeks before school started again. My escape with Allen to see his life had to come to an end and I needed to get back to my life and try to put it in some kind of order.

No one in the Green family wanted to see me leave. They urged me to stay to hunt moose with Allen and then go back to Oregon with him when he returned for school in September. But they sensed that I had some things to attend to in Oregon and they held a little going-away party for me. I received a bright red pair of suspenders with the words "Alaska Fisherman" embossed on them, a cap that said "Alaska" on it, and a coffee mug that had the image of a canvasback duck painted on it.

After goodbyes and hugs, Allen and I drove alone in his father's pickup to the airport in St. Mary's. We drove with relative silence between our teeth, speaking only about surface matters such as to point out a flock of cranes or a cloud of mosquitoes. I was leaving Alaska with far more than I brought with me. For one thing, Allen packed nine fresh silver salmon on ice in freezer boxes for me to take home. More importantly, I was leaving Alaska with an experience that very few from the "Lower Forty-eight"—"Outside"—ever had. I had lived with Yup'ik Eskimos in their own environment and experienced their culture.

By now, I came to know each Green family member as an individual and understood each of their passions as well as their perceptions. Allen, Clara, Clyde and their siblings were all bilingual and bicultural. They could converse in both English and Yup'ik, so comfortably that they easily could switch between the two languages in the same conversation without missing anything in translation. They could communicate in Yup'ik with the elders, such as their parents, as well as in English with the third generation, their children, nieces and nephews. Allen, Clara, and their older brother Philip were passionate about the youth in the Yup'ik communities. They wanted the youth to understand and to gain a firm foundation in the Yup'ik language and cultural traditions while being able to thrive in the macro-modern world. Other second generation members, such as Clyde, simply wanted to live the old ways and dealt with their frustrations with the changes, by drowning them with alcohol and drugs. The elders knew cultural change was coming, and sometimes felt disinherited that the "old ways" may be dying, that their grandchildren showed little long-term interest in learning the Yup'ik language and culture. This may be a typical response between generations. Russell Baker, in his 1982 Pulitzer Prize winning autobiography, *Growing Up*, summarized his thoughts on generational transfer of knowledge with his experiences with his mother sinking into dementia, "Children rarely want to know who their parents were before they were parents, and when age finally stirs their curiosity, there is no parent left to tell them" (6).

I arrived in Alaska ignorant of boats, rough open waters, and was immersed

Assorted Green family members traveling on the river. Dan Syljuberget is at the tiller. His college classmate, Clara Green, is on the lower right side of the photograph and looking at her brother, Allen Green, the photographer. Dan, Allen, and Clara were classmates at Western Oregon State College.

in a culture that previous to attending college was quite foreign to me. With the additional ten pounds added to my frame, I was leaving Alaska as a seasoned commercial fishing deckhand for a Yukon River family and with an inside look at the contemporary life and culture of riverine Yup'ik Eskimos. I was also leaving Alaska with memories of experiences that would affect me for the rest of my life and made some important decisions about my life, about my future career. I wanted to learn more about the Yup'ik culture, its changes and how it would respond to further changes. And I decided that I wanted to write and to learn to approach life as Papa Joseph did—to watch, listen, and then act. This became a personal covenant for the rest of my life.

As we walked towards the little plane that would shuttle me three hours to Anchorage, Allen stopped me and hugged me. He summed up everything I was thinking, "Dan. We have an old saying in Alaska. When you leave Alaska, you leave part of you behind."

AFTERWORD

Mike and Zach came with Allen and Clyde to Oregon in September. Allen wanted the boys to experience a taste of "outside." Neither boy had ever been outside of Alaska, so the trip to Oregon was quite an experience for them. They were overwhelmed with culture shock; they especially could not get over the cars, the highways, and the traffic. The hustle and bustle of western Oregon was almost too much for them.

The first thing that Mike wanted to see was an apple tree. As we drove from the airport in Portland to Monmouth, I spied an apple tree in a field as we neared Monmouth. I stopped the car and let the boys out. They scrambled over the barb-wire fence with no injuries and over to the tree. Fourteen-year-old Zach was able to reach an apple and pluck it from the tree, but frustrated little Mike was too short to reach one. Zach offered to grab one for him. But Mike protested by demanding. "No. I want to get one. Come lift." Allen ran over and gave his nephew a boost so that he could pull a fresh apple from the tree. The boys were also excited to see the domestic animals they heard about in school. They had never before seen sheep, cattle, hogs, and horses until visiting Oregon.

Good-looking and charismatic Zach enjoyed a great deal of attention from the girls at high school in nearby Independence that fall. So much attention that the "Zachary Green Fan Club" was heartbroken when it became known that homesick Zach was not returning to Oregon from Alaska after Christmas break. Despite his popularity, Zach really missed his friends, his brother, sister, and father in Mountain Village. Clyde also stayed in Alaska after Christmas break because the pressures of school were too much for him.

Mike, who was more like a son than a nephew to Allen, became quite popular at Campus Elementary. Stories spread throughout the local kids about the legendary feats of strength of the quiet Eskimo boy from Mountain Village, Alaska. None of us who knew Mike were surprised at how strong and athletic he was when compared to the other Monmouth children his age because he had been competing with his older brother and older cousins all of his life. In the group of kids that he played and fought with in Alaska, he was the youngest and smallest by several years. After Christmas break, he alone shared the apartment with Allen.

After several years of teaching in Russian Mission, Alaska, Allen and Clara returned to teach in their home community of Mountain Village. Clara taught kindergarten for several years before marrying and moving to teach in one of the coastal villages. Allen became the lead teacher in Mountain Village, which is like an assistant to the school principal. Both Clara and Allen settled well into the teaching profession within their culture.

Choosing to get his children away from the environment in Mountain Village, Phillip moved his family to Anchorage where he worked many years as a hospital administrator. In Anchorage, his children were not teased and ridiculed for doing well in academics by their peers, nor were they pressured as much to drink alcohol as they were in Mountain Village. Instead they were encouraged to excel in a positive lifestyle in Anchorage.

Allen's oldest brothers, Leonard and Frank swore off a dependence on alcohol, and became completely sober, abstaining from alcohol. They started a local taxi service which often made runs to and from nearby St. Mary's, on the gravel road between the two villages in the summer months, and on the frozen Yukon River during the winter months. Allen and his older brothers became closer in recent years.

Clyde voluntarily admitted himself to an alcohol and drug treatment center in Bethel. His treatment was reportedly successful.

One of Allen's younger sister's, Joy, completed a degree in elementary education from the University of Alaska in Fairbanks. That made four children in this amazing family of Joseph and Arlene Green to achieve university degrees. Allen and Clara's youngest sister, MaryAnn, completed a two-year college program in secretarial work and currently works for the Lower Yukon School District; the district offices are housed in Mountain Village.

In the years that have passed since Allen bade me goodbye at the tiny airport in St. Mary's, Alaska, I have often thought about his words to me as we parted. The experiences of knowing Allen and his family and sharing their lives in the brush of Alaska have had long lasting effects on my life. It is as if those parting words of his, "when you leave Alaska, you leave a part of you behind," were prophetically true. I remembered Allen's early months at WOSC and the culture shock he must have felt. I knew what that felt like now that I had shared his world in Yup'ik Alaska. I knew the out-of-place feeling, the confusion, and the sensory overload from taking in all the newness.

When I returned to Oregon from Alaska that August, I experienced culture shock all over again and nearly as acutely as my first few days in Alaska. After having lived in Alaska with people who live fairly close to nature, I had a new perspective of my world that was now a little askew from my previous views.

I was amazed at the hustle-bustle of our modern urban world. Everyone seemed to be in such a hurry. Further, the artificiality of our modern urban world overwhelmed me during the first few days back in western Oregon. In Alaska, especially at fish camp on the island in the middle of the Yukon River, everything around me seemed cohesive, to flow together smoothly, especially the colors and tones of things. The human-made objects, such as boats and shacks, perhaps because they were painted in earth tones, seemed to blend well with their natural environment. Even the flashes of pickups and ATVs seemed muted for some reason in Mountain Village.

By contrast, during my first days back from the Alaskan bush, in the airports in Anchorage and Seattle, then on the drive from Seattle to my parent's home in Silverton, Oregon with my Uncle Floyd, garish, bright colors seemed to assault my eyes everywhere I looked. Everywhere, on the seats of chairs in restaurants, on billboards and storefronts, and on the items on the shelves in those stores; all seemed to be an affront. So overwhelming was the gaudy brightness of my world that shortly after I was reunited with my family at our home in Silverton, I insisted on a trip up to nearby Silver Falls State Park, a beautiful, huge wooded tract of land in the foothills of the Cascade Mountains. The park contains miles of trails that wind down to the forest, in and around, and even behind the waterfalls of Silver Creek.

The garish artificiality of my world was blinding and nauseating to me. My parents' home was dominated by rust-orange carpet throughout. I couldn't stand it. I felt horribly claustrophobic. I had a few more small hints in those first few days back in Oregon of the culture shock that Allen, Clara, and Donnie and the rest of the Green family experienced when they first came to Oregon. Because I was, after all, back on my native grounds, the culture shock and the blinding gaudiness of my world that banged my eyes those first few days after returning to

Oregon, lessened within a week. Other effects from my experience of living with riverine, Yup'ik Eskimos in rural Alaska have never left me.

Even before meeting Allen, I had always held a keen interest in learning about and knowing people from different cultures. Knowing Allen intimately served to heighten this curiosity. More so now, I gravitate toward people from cultural backgrounds other than my own Anglo-Saxon, Midwestern, middle class, Judeo-Christian upbringing. Likewise, people seemed to be attracted to me so that I become, in a sense, a liaison between my culture and other cultures. I walk in two worlds now too. Perhaps though, and even more than a heightened multicultural awareness, my relationship with Allen and sharing a brief part of his life with him in Alaska made me look at life a little more differently from before. I notice the simple beauty in life perhaps more now. Thoreau's "simplicity, simplicity, simplicity"—his writings extolling the virtues of simple living—have more meaning now. We are, as he wrote, too caught up in the "quiet desperation" of everyday life, and too often veer away from "living deliberately."

Spending a summer gathering food from nature by netting salmon, shooting waterfowl and beaver from the river, picking salmonberries and rhubarbs from the tundra, putting up dry fish for the following winter—the simple acts of working directly in nature to provide sustenance for the entire coming year, and the enormous physical and emotional stress involved in these harvests somehow made things like insurance, war, taxes, career pressures, and the menagerie of material goods that we seem to feel as necessary—a little less important.

I did leave a part of me behind in Alaska, perhaps the inhibitions of my youth. However, I brought much more back with me, including maturity, a heightened cultural awareness and strong reminders to focus on simplicity in life rather than to be addicted to the hurry-up-and-wait complexity of our contemporary, technological society. I also came back with a great desire to return. Perhaps, after all, that is what Allen meant when he said, "We have an old saying in Alaska—when you leave, you leave part of you behind."

Works Cited

Baker, Russell. *Growing up.* New York: Congdon and Weed, 1982.

Barker, James H. *Always Getting Ready, Upterrlainarluta: Yup'ik Eskimo Subsistence in Southwest Alaska.* Seattle: University of Washington Press, 1993.

This book focuses on the riverine subsistence culture of these people in a well-written essay format with many fascinating black and white photographs.

Collier, Catherine. *Teacher's Supplement to Accompany the Yup'ik-as-a-Second Language Curriculum.* Juneau, AK: Kuskokwim Community College, 1977.

Jacobson, Steven A. *Yup'ik Eskimo Dictionary.* Fairbanks: Alaska Native Language Center, University of Alaska, 1984.

The only one of its kind.

Morgan, Lael. *Alaska's Native People.* Edmonds, WA: Alaska Geographic Society, 1979.

Also an excellent source; contains a 47-page section of text and color photographs on Yup'ik Eskimos. This book also includes an overall history of the peopling of Alaska.

ABOUT DAN
SYLJUBERGET

B orn and raised in Aberdeen, South Dakota until moving to Oregon at age 16, Dan Syljuberget (Sil-you-berg-it) has been an educator in South Dakota and Wyoming schools, colleges, and universities for over two decades. In addition to his Alaska experiences, Syljuberget earned his Doctorate in Education and currently lives and works as an educator in Wyoming while maintaining close ties to family scattered throughout the western and central United States and Canada.

An outdoor enthusiast, Syljuberget enjoys hiking, wildlife observation, and bicycling. He occasionally sings, plays the guitar, and writes nonfiction. His writings follow his passion for three main themes: 1) the relationship between humans and nature; 2) Indigenous American cultural continuity and sociological transition; and 3) the narrative voice, such as story-telling, as a powerful research and learning tool.

35061824R00096

Made in the USA
Middletown, DE
18 September 2016